FINAL –*Y*

IN NON-MANICHAEAN PARTHIAN AND THE PROTO-PARTHIAN 'RHYTMIC LAW'

STUDIA IRANICA. CAHIER 52

FINAL –*Y* IN NON-MANICHAEAN PARTHIAN AND THE PROTO-PARTHIAN 'RHYTMIC LAW'

JUANJO FERRER-LOSILLA

PUBLIÉ AVEC LE CONCOURS DU PROJET 'AVESTAN DIGITAL ARCHIVE' (REF. FFI2011-27523), FINANCÉ PAR LE MINISTERIO DE ECONOMÍA Y COMPETITIVIDAD (ESPAGNE)

ASSOCIATION POUR L'AVANCEMENT DES ÉTUDES IRANIENNES

PARIS 2014

Illustration de la couverture :
Narseh à Paikuli, bloc parthe e6
(Missione Archeologica Italiana nel Kurdistan Iracheno [MAIKI]),
avec l'autorisation de Carlo Cereti et Gianfilippo Terribili
©Sulaimaniyah Museum

LES *CAHIERS DE STUDIA IRANICA*
sont publiés par
L'ASSOCIATION POUR L'AVANCEMENT DES ÉTUDES IRANIENNES

Direction des *Cahiers de Studia Iranica*
Ph. Gignoux et R. Gyselen

DIFFUSION
Peeters PRESS, Bondgenotenlaan 153, P.B. 41
B-3000 Leuven (Belgique)

ISSN 0993 - 8699
ISBN 978-2-910640-38-5

PREFACE

A final *–y* may appear at the end of some words both in Inscriptional Middle Persian and in Inscriptional Parthian. This issue has been the subject of much discussion from the earliest phases of Iranian Linguistics through to the present day (Theodor Nöldeke [1880] – Paolo Milizia [2011]). However, current research on the presence or absence of this final sign and the historical or orthographical justifications given for it have focused mainly on the Southwestern variant (Middle Persian). The most recent and exhaustive study of Inscriptional Middle Persian final *–y* has been carried out by Philip Huyse (2003), who laid down the basic guidelines explaining the presence or absence of *–y* in this language: the final *–y* appears in monosyllable nouns and after polysyllables following a short vowelled syllable, whereas it is absent in polysyllables following a long vowelled syllable. Nevertheless, regarding the use of the final *–y* in Inscriptional Parthian, Huyse (2003: 37) expresses his obfuscation in the following words: "Le *y* final parthe est apparemment soumis à d'autres règles qu'en moyen-perse, sans qu'on puisse établir de véritable justification pour sa présence ou son absence".

Despite the doubts expressed by Philip Huyse, I have sought to explain the use and function of the final *–y* in Inscriptional Parthian, based on a method similiar to his own for Inscriptional Middle Persian: collecting and classifying the material according to the number of syllables in each word (monosyllables and polysyllables) and to the syllabic weight (heavy or light) of the syllable preceding the final *–y*. After organizing the vocabulary in this way, I provide a history of the Parthian nominal inflection that seems to yield a suitable explanation for the presence or absence of the final *–y* on certain words in its inscriptional variant.

This work is the outcome of my own research on the Middle Persian and Parthian verbal forms in my PhD dissertation. During this investigation, I have stated that no Parthian verbal form has the final *–y* (except for the optative ending ⟨-ndy⟩ *-ēndē*), while several forms do so in Inscriptional Middle Persian. On this basis, I have extended the analysis to the nominal inflexion, since it seemed rather strange that such similar languages as Parthian and Middle Persian follow a convention that is so different in their use of the sign *–y* at the end of some words.

Since the start of my research, I have reported parts of my results on different occasions: at the *1st Meeting of the Sociedad Española de Iranología*–SEI (Salamanca-September 2010), at the *7th European*

Conference of Iranian Studies–ECIS7 (Cracow-September 2011), and at the *1st International Conference of Iranian Languages and Dialects: Past and Present* (Tehran-June 2012). This has allowed me to refine and enrich some of my initial findings. I wish to express my gratitude to some of my colleagues, namely, Desmond Durkin-Meisterernst and Thomas Jügel, for their comments and textual corrections; Ana Agud, Jaime Martínez and Irene de la Fuente, for their proofreading and style check, and particularly Alberto Cantera, for the numerous discussions on the history of the nominal inflexion, and for his commitment to this study, which has allowed it to eventually see the light of day. The project he is leading, and where I have been working in recent years, the *Avestan Digital Archive* (ADA), sponsored by Spain's Ministry of the Economy and Competitiveness and the Regional Government, the *Junta*, of Castilla y León (Spain), has provided the context in which I have been able to pursue this work.

Finally, I would like to thank Philip Gignoux and Rika Gyselen, editors of the Series "Cahiers de Studia Iranica", for having accepted this study in their collection.

Juanjo Ferrer
November 2014
University of Salamanca

TABLE OF CONTENTS

BIBLIOGRAPHY

Back 1978 — M. Back, *Die Sassanidischen Staatsinschriften – Studien zur Orthographie und Phonologie des Mittelpersischen der Inschriften zusammen mit einem etymologischen Index des mittelpersischen Wortgutes und einem Textcorpus der behandelten Inschriften* [Acta Iranica, 18], Leiden: Brill, 1978.

Back 1988 — M. Back, "Kirdegān", in *A Green Leaf (Barg-i sabz). Papers in Honour of Professor Jes P. Asmussen* [Acta Iranica, 28, Deuxième série, Hommages et Opera Minora, 12], J. Duchesne-Guillemin, W. Sundermann et F. Vahman (eds.), Leiden: Brill, 1988, p. 45-60.

Bailey 1943 — H. W. Bailey, "Caucasica", *Journal of the Royal Asiatic Society*, 75, 1943, p. 1-5.

Basharin 2011 — P. Basharin, "Nominal Endings in Middle Persian Ideograms", unpublished [paper presented in the *7th European Conference of Iranian Studies (ECIS 7)*, hold in Cracow from September 7th till September 10th 2011].

Bartholomae 1920 — Ch. Bartholomae, "Zum sassanidischen Recht. III", *Sitzungsberichte der Heidelberger Akademie der Wissenschaften*, Heidelberg: Universitätsverlag C. Winter, 1920, p. 3-75.

Brandenstein/Mayrhofer 1964 — W. Brandestein and M. Mayrhofer, *Handbuch des Altpersischen*, Wiesbaden: Harrassowitz, 1964.

Brunner 1972 — Ch. J. Brunner, [Review of] "Frye, R. N. (ed.), *The Parthian and Middle Persian Inscriptions of Dura-Europos*, Corpus inscriptionum iranicarum. Part III. Pahlavi inscriptions. Vol. III Dura-Europos", *Journal of the American Oriental Society*, 92-4, 1972, p. 492-497.

Brunner 1974 — Ch. J. Brunner, "The Middle Persian Inscription of the Priest Kirdēr at Naqš-i Rustam", in *Near Eastern numismatics, iconography, epigraphy and history – studies in honor of George C. Miles*, D. K. Kouymjian (ed.), Beirut: American University of Beirut, 1974, p. 97-113.

Cantera 1999 — A. Cantera, "Die Stellung der Sprache der Pahlavi-Übersetzung des Avesta innerhalb des Mittelpersischen", *Studia Iranica*, 28/2, 1999, p. 173-204.

Cantera 2006 — A. Cantera, [Review of] "Huyse, Philip, Le *y* final dans les inscriptions moyen-perses et la loi rythmique Proto-moyen-perse", *Studia Iranica*, 35, 2006, p. 148-153.

Cantera 2009 A. Cantera, "On the history of the Middle Persian nominal inflection", in *Exegisti monumenta. Festschrift in honour of Nicholas Sims-Williams* [Iranica, 17], W. Sundermann, A. Hintze and Fr. de Blois (eds.), Wiesbaden: Harrassowitz, 2009, p. 17-30.

Cereti/Terribili 2014 C. G. Cereti and G. Terribili, "The Middle Persian and Parthian Inscriptions on the Paikuli Tower – New Blocks and Preliminary Studies", *Iranica Antiqua*, 49, 2014, p. 347-412.

Cheung 2007 J. Cheung, *Etymological Dictionary of the Iranian Verb* [Leiden Indo-European Etymological Dictionary Series 2, ed. by A. Lubotsky], Leiden: Brill, 2007.

Cowley 1919 A. Cowley, "The Pahlavi documents from Avroman", *Journal of the Royal Asiatic Society*, 1919, p. 147-154.

Diakonoff/Livshits 1977 I. M. Diakonoff and V. A. Livshits, *Parthian Economic Documents from Nisa.* Texts I [p. 1-80] (ed. by D. N. MacKenzie), Corpus Inscriptionum Iranicarum Part II *Inscriptions of the Seleucid and Parthian Periods and of Eastern Iran and Central Asia*, Vol. II, Parthian, London: Lund Humphries, 1977.

Diakonoff/Livshits 1998 I. M. Diakonoff and V. A. Livshits, *Parthian Economic Documents from Nisa.* Texts I [p. 81-160] (ed. by D. N. MacKenzie), Corpus Inscriptionum Iranicarum Part II *Inscriptions of the Seleucid and Parthian Periods and of Eastern Iran and Central Asia*, Vol. II, Parthian, London: Lund Humphries, 1988.

Diakonoff/Livshits 1999 I. M. Diakonoff and V. A. Livshits, *Parthian Economic Documents from Nisa.* Texts I [p. 161-215] (ed. by D. N. MacKenzie), Corpus Inscriptionum Iranicarum Part II *Inscriptions of the Seleucid and Parthian Periods and of Eastern Iran and Central Asia*, Vol. II, Parthian, London: Lund Humphries, 1999.

Durkin-Meisterernst 2000 D. Durkin-Meisterernst, "Zum partischen Verbum", in *Indoarisch, Iranisch und die Indogermanistik – Arbeitstagung der Idg. Gesellschaft vom 2. bis 5. Oktober 1997 in Erlangen*, B. Forssman and R. Plath (eds.), Wiesbaden: Reichert, 2000, p. 75-88.

Durkin-Meisterernst 2004 D. Durkin-Meisterernst, *Dictionary of Manichaean Middle Persian and Parthian* [Dictionary of Manichaean Texts III: Texts from Central Asia and China 1, Corpus Fontium Manichaeorum Subsidia], Turnhout: Brepols, 2004.

Durkin-Meisterernst 2014 D. Durkin-Meisterernst, *Grammatik des Westmittel-iranischen (Parthisch und Mittelpersisch)* [Veröffentlichungen Zur Iranistik, 73], Wien: Verlag der Österreichischen Akademie der Wissenschaften, 2014.

Ferrer-Losilla 2010 J. J. Ferrer-Losilla, "Ergatividad y complementos fonéticos en las inscripciones sasánidas: un problema de concordancia en la tercera persona del plural", *Boletín de la Sociedad Española de Iranología*, 1, 2010, p. 87-100.

Ferrer-Losilla 2013 J. J. Ferrer-Losilla, *Las desinencias verbales en iranio medio occidental/ Western Middle Iranian Personal Endings*, unpublished [Ph.D. dissertation at the Facultad de Filología, Universidad de Salamanca, 22 May 2013, avalaible at http://ada.usal.es/img/pdf/tesisFerrer_2013.pdf].

Frye 1968 R. N. Frye (ed.), "The Parthian and Middle Persian Inscriptions of Dura-Europos", *Corpus inscriptionum iranicarum. Part III. Pahlavi inscriptions. Vol. III Dura-Europos*, London: Percy Lund, Humphries and Co.Ltd., 1968.

Gauthiot 1961a R. Gauthiot, "Du pluriel persan en -hâ", *Mémoires de la Societé Linguistique de Paris*, 20, 1961, p. 71-76.

Gauthiot 1961b R. Gauthiot, "De l'accent d'intensité en perse", *Mémoires de la Societé Linguistique de Paris*, 20, 1961, p. 1-25.

Ghilain 1939 A. Ghilain, *Essai sur la langue parthe – son système verbal d'après les textes manichéens du Turkestan oriental*, Leuven: Institut Orientaliste, 1939 [reprint 1966].

Gignoux 1972a Ph. Gignoux, *Glossaire des Inscriptions Pehlevies et Parthes*. [Corpus Inscriptionum Iranicarum, Supplementary Series Vol. 1], London: Lund Humphries, 1972.

Gignoux 1972b Ph. Gignoux, "L'inscription de Kirdīr à Naqš-i Rustam", *Studia Iranica*, 1, 1972, p. 177-205.

Gignoux 1991a Ph. Gignoux, *Les Quatre Inscriptions du Mage Kirdīr – Textes et Concordances* [Studia Iranica, Cahier 9], Leuven: Association pour l'avancement des études iraniennes, 1991.

Gignoux 1991b Ph. Gignoux, "D'Abnūn à Māhān: étude de deux inscriptions sassanides", *Studia Iranica*, 20/1, 1991, p. 9-22.

Gignoux/Gyselen 1982 Ph. Gignoux and R. Gyselen, *Sceaux sassanides de diverses collections privées* [Studia Iranica, Cahier 1], Leuven: Association pour l'avancement des études iraniennes, 1982.

Henning 1933 W. B. Henning, "Das Verbum des Mittelpersischen der Turfanfragmente", *Zeitschrift für Indologie und Iranistik*, 9, 1933, p. 158-253.

Henning 1944 W. B. Henning, "Bráhman", *Transactions of the Philological Society*, 1944, p. 108-118.

Henning 1948 W. B. Henning, "The date of the Sogdian Ancient Letters", *Bulletin of the School of Oriental and African Studies*, 12, 1948, p. 601-615.

Henning 1952a W. B. Henning, "The monuments and inscriptions of Tang-i Sarvak", *Asia Major*, 2, 1952, p. 151-178.

Henning 1952b W. B. Henning, "A Farewell to the Khagan of the Aq-Aqatärān", *Bulletin of the School of Oriental and African Studies*, 14/3, 1952, p. 501-522.

Henning 1953 W. B. Henning, "A new Parthian inscription (Plate V)", *Journal of the Royal Asiatic Society*, 85, 1953, p. 131-136.

Henning 1958 W. B. Henning, "Mitteliranisch", in *Handbuch der Orientalistik – Iranistik, erster Abschnitt: Linguistik*, B. Spuler (ed.), Leiden-Köln: Brill, 1958, p. 20-129.

Henning 1960 W. B. Henning, "The Bactrian inscription", *Bulletin of the School of Oriental and African Studies*, 23, 1960, p. 47-55.

Henning 1961 W. B. Henning, "A Sassanian silver bowl from Georgia", *Bulletin of the School of Oriental and African Studies*, 24, 1961, p. 353-356.

Henning 1965 W. B. Henning, "Surkh-Kotal und Kaniṣka", Zeitschrift *der Deutschen Morgenländischen Gesellschaft*, 115, 1965, p. 75-87.

Herzfeld 1935 E. Herzfeld, "Medisch und Parthisch", *Archaeologische Mitteilungen aus Iran*, 7, 1935, p. 9-64. [Quoted *apud* Sims-Williams (2004)]

Hoberman 1988 R. D. Hoberman, "The history of the Modern Aramaic Pronouns and Pronominal Suffixes", *Journal of the Asiatic Oriental Society*, 108/4, 1988, p. 557-575.

Humbach 1978 H. Humbach, *The Sassanian Inscription of Paikuli, Part 1, Supplement to Herzfeld's Paikuli*, Wiesbaden: Reichert, 1978.

Humbach/Skjærvø 1980 H. Humbach and P. O. Skjærvø, *The Sassanian Inscription of Paikuli, Part 2, Synoptic Tables*, Wiesbaden: Reichert, 1980.

Huyse 1999 Ph. Huyse, *Die dreisprachige Inschrift Šābuhrs I. an der Ka'ba-i Zardušt (ŠKZ) Band 1 + 2* [Corpus Inscriptionum Iranicarum, Part 3: Pahlavi Inscriptions, Vol. I: Royal Inscriptions with their Parthian and Greek Versions], London: Corpus Inscriptionum Iranicarum and School of Oriental and African Studies, 1999.

Huyse 2003 — Ph. Huyse, *Le* y *final dans les inscriptions moyen-perses et la 'loi rythmique' proto-moyen-perse* [Studia Iranica, Cahier 29], Paris: Association pour l'avancement des études iraniennes, 2003.

Huyse 2005 — Ph. Huyse, "Ein erneuter Deutungsversuch für den Übergang vom Schluss-*y* der mittelpersischen Inschriften zum Endstrich im Buchpahlavi (6.-7. Jh.)", in *Languages of Iran: Past and Present. Iranian Studies in memoriam David Neil MacKenzie* [Iranica 8], D. Weber (ed.), Wiesbaden: Harrassowitz, 2005, p. 51-68.

Jügel 2010 — Th. Jügel, *Konkordanz der Kirdīr-Inschriften* [available online on the TITUS webpage: http://titus.uni-frankfurt.de/personal/tjuegel/kirdir.pdf].

Jügel 2014 — Th. Jügel, "On the linguistic history of Kurdish", *Kurdish Studies*, 2/2, 2014, p. 123-142.

Jügel Forthc. — Th. Jügel, *Die Entwicklung der Ergativkonstruktion im Alt- und Mitteliranischen – Eine korpusbasierte Untersuchung zu Kasus, Kongruenz und Satzbau* [2 Volumes], to appear in *Iranica*, M. Macuch (ed.), Wiesbaden: Harrassowitz. [Original Ph.D. dissertation at the Institut für Vergleichende Sprachwissenschaften der Universität Frankfurt am Main, 2012].

Klingenschmitt 2000 — G. Klingenschmitt, "Mittelpersisch", in *Indoarisch, Iranisch und die Indogermanistik. Arbeitstagung der Indogermanischen Gesellschaft vom 2. bis 5. Oktober 1997 in Erlangen*, B. Forssman and R. Plath (eds.), Wiesbaden: Reichert, 2000, p. 191-229.

Korn 2009 — A. Korn, "Lengthening of *i* and *u* in Persian", in *Exegisti monumenta, Festschrift in Honour of Nicholas Sims-Williams*, W. Sundermann, A. Hintze and Fr. de Blois (eds.), Wiesbaden: Harrassowitz, 2009, p. 197-213.

Korn 2010 — A. Korn, "Parthian *ž*", *Bulletin of the School of Oriental and African Studies*, 73, 2010, p. 415-436.

Korn 2013 — A. Korn, "Footnotes on a Parthian sound change", *Bulletin of the School of Oriental and African Studies*, 76, 2013, p. 99-110.

MacKenzie 1971 — D. N. MacKenzie, *A Concise Pahlavi Dictionary*, London: Oxford University Press, 1971.

MacKenzie 1978 — D. N. MacKenzie, "Shapur's shooting", *Bulletin of the School of Oriental and African Studies*, 41/3, 1978, p. 499-511. [Reprinted in MacKenzie (1999): vol. 1, p. 73-82].

MacKenzie 1982 — D. N. MacKenzie, [Review of] "Back M. (1978), *Die sassanidischen Staatsinschriften*", *Indogermanische Forschungen*, 87, 1982, p. 280-297.

MacKenzie 1985 D. N. MacKenzie, "Avroman documents", *Encyclopaedia Iranica* I, 1985, p. 111ab.

MacKenzie 1999 D. N. MacKenzie, *Iranica Diversa*, C. G. Cereti and L. Paul (eds.), Rome: Instituto Italiano per l'Africa e l'Oriente [Serie Orientale Roma, vol. LXXXIV, 1-2], 1999.

Meillet 1900 A. Meillet, "La déclinaison et l'accent d'intensité en perse", *Journal Asiatique*, 15, 1900, p. 254-277.

Milizia 2011 P. Milizia, "Considerazioni sul segno di fine di parola del Mediopersiano epigrafico", *Segno e Testo, International Journal of Manuscripts and Text Transmission*, 9, 2011, p. 63-92.

Minns 1915 E. H. Minss, "Parchments of the Parthian Period from Avroman in Kurdistan", *Journal of Hellenic Studies*, 35/1, 1915, p. 22-65.

Morano 1990 E. Morano, "Contributi all'interpretazione della bilingue greco-partica dell'Eracle di Seleucia", in *Proceedings of the First European Conference of Iranian Studies, Pt. 1. Old and Middle Iranian Studies*, G. Gnoli and A. Panaino (eds.), Roma: Serie Orientale Roma LXXVII/1, 1990, p. 229-238.

Nawabi 1993 M. Nawabi, "A Small Parthian Inscription from the Nayyeri Collection", *Zeitschrift der Deutschen Morgenländischen Gesellschaft*, 143, 1993, p. 192-193.

Nyberg 1923 H. S. Nyberg, "The Pahlavi Documents from Avromān", *Monde Oriental*, 17, 1923, p. 182-230.

Nyberg 1974 H. S. Nyberg, *A Manual of Pahlavi II – Ideograms, Glossary, Abbreviations, Index, Grammatical Survey, Corrigenda Part I*, Wiesbaden: Harrassowitz, 1974.

Pat-El 2008 N. Pat-El, "Historical Syntax of Aramaic: A Note on Subordination", in *Aramaic in its Historical and Linguistic Setting*, H. Gzella and M. L. Folmer (eds.), Wiesbaden: Harrassowitz, 2008, p. 55-76.

Perkins 1959 A. Perkins (ed.), *The excavations at Dura-Europos*, Final Report V, Part I, 1959.

Rastorgueva/Molčanova 1981 V. S. Rastorgueva and E. K. Molčanova, "Parfjanskij Jazyk", in *Osnovy Iranskogo Jazykoznanija*, V. I. Abaev *et al.* (eds.), Moskau: NAUK, 1981, p. 147-232.

Schmitt 1973 R. Schmitt, "Reversindex zum Glossar der mittelpersischen und parthischen Steininschriften", *Indo-Iranian Journal*, 15, 1973, p. 241-263.

Shaked 1994 S. Shaked, "Two Parthian ostraca from Nippur", *Bulletin of the School of Oriental and African Studies*, 57, 1994, p. 208-212.

Sims-Williams 1979 N. Sims-Williams, "Parthian sound-change", *Bulletin of the School of Oriental and African Studies*, 42/1, 1979, p. 133-136.

Sims-Williams 1981 N. Sims-Williams, "Notes on Manichaean Middle Persian Morphology", *Studia Iranica*, 10/2, 1981, p. 165-176.

Sims-Williams 1984 N. Sims-Williams, "The Sogdian 'Rhythmic Law'", in *Middle Iranian Studies. Proceedings of the International Symposium Organized by the Katholieke Universiteit Leuven from the 17th to the 20th of May 1982*, W. Skalmowski and A. VanTongerloo (eds.), Leuven: Orientalia Lovaniensia Analecta 16, 1984, p. 203-215.

Sims-Williams 1990 N. Sims-Williams, "Chotano-Sogdica II: Aspects of the Development of Nominal Morphology in Khotanese and Sogdian", in *Proceedings of the First European Conference of Iranian Studies, Pt. 1. Old and Middle Iranian Studies*, G. Gnoli and A. Panaino (eds.), Roma: Serie Orientale Roma LXXVII/1, 1990, p. 275-296.

Sims-Williams 2004 N. Sims-Williams, "The Parthian abstract suffix *-yft*", in *Indo-European Perspectives. Studies in Honour of Anna Morpurgo Davies*, J. H. W. Penney (ed.), Oxford and New York: Oxford University Press, 2004, p. 538-547.

Sims-Williams 2007 N. Sims-Williams, *Bactrian documents from Northern Afghanistan II: Letters and Buddhist Texts* [Studies in the Khalili Collection, vol. III; Corpus Inscriptionum Iranicarum, Part II : Inscriptions of the Seleucid and Parthian Periods and of Eastern Iran and Central Asia], London: The Nour Foundation in association with Azimuth Editions, 2007.

Skjærvø 1976 P. O. Skjærvø, "Sogdian notes", *Acta Orientalia*, 37, 1976, p. 111-116.

Skjærvø 1983a P. O. Skjærvø, "Case in Inscriptional Middle Persian, Inscriptional Parthian and the Pahlavi Psalter" [two parts], *Studia Iranica*, 12/1, 1983, p. 47-62; *Studia Iranica*, 12/2, 1983, p. 151-181.

Skjærvø 1983b P. O. Skjærvø, *The Sassanian Inscription of Paikuli, part 3.1: Restored text and translation*, Wiesbaden: Reichert, 1983.

Skjærvø 1983c P. O. Skjærvø, *The Sassanian Inscription of Paikuli, part 3.2: Commentary*, Wiesbaden: Reichert, 1983.

Skjærvø 1989 P. O. Skjærvø, "Verbal Ideograms and the Imperfect in Middle Persian and Parthian", in *Études Irano-aryennes offertes à Gilbert Lazard, réunies par Charles-Henri de Fouchécour and Philippe Gignoux* [Studia Iranica, Cahier

7], Paris: Association pour l'avancement des éstudes iraniennes, 1989, p. 333-354.

Skjærvø 1990 — P. O. Skjærvø, "A Copy of the Hajiabad Inscription in the Babylonian Collection, Yale", *Bulletin of the Asia Institute*, N.S. 4, 1990, p. 289-293.

Skjærvø 1995 — P. O. Skjærvø, "Aramaic in Iran", *ARAM* 7 [1997/8] (*Palmyra and the Aramaeans*), 1995, p. 283-318.

Skjærvø 1997 — P. O. Skjærvø, "On the Middle Persian Imperfect", in *Syntaxe des langues indo-iraniennes anciennes – Coloque international, Sitges Barcelona, 4.-5. Mai 1993*, É. Pirart (ed.), Barcelona: Ausa (Aula Orientalis Supplementa 6), 1997, p. 161-188.

Skjærvø 2009 — P. O. Skjærvø, "Middle West Iranian", in *The Iranian Languages*, G. Windfuhr (ed.), London/New York: Routledge, 2009, p. 196-278.

Tedesco 1921 — P. Tedesco, Dialektologie *der westiranischen Turfantexte*, *Monde Oriental*, 15, 1921, p. 184-257.

Werba 1982 — C. Werba, *Die arischen Personennamen und ihre Träger bei den Alexanderhistorikern (Studien zur iranischen Anthroponomastik)* [Ph.D. dissertation at the Geisteswissenschaftlichen Fakultät der Universität Wien].

Windfuhr 1975 — G. Windfuhr, [Review of] "Gignoux Ph. (1972), *Glossaire des Inscriptions Pehlevies et Parthes*", *Journal of the American Oriental Society*, 95/2, 1975, p. 296-298.

Zimmer 1984 — S. Zimmer, "Iran. *baga* — ein Gottesname?", *Münchener Studien zur Sprachwissenschaft*, 43, 1984, p. 187-215.

ABBREVIATIONS AND SYMBOLS

Abbreviations and signs

abl.	ablative
acc.	accusative
adj.	adjective
Aram.	Aramaic
Av.	Avestan
Bact.	Bactrian
cf.	*confer(te)* / check
corrig.	*corrigendum* / to be changed
e.g.	*exempli gratia* / for example
f.	feminine
fn.	footnote
gen.	genitive
Gr.	Greek
IE	Indo-European
IIr.	Indo-Iranian
IMP	Inscriptional Middle Persian
Impf.	imperfect
Impv.	imperative
Ind.	indicative
IPa	Inscriptional Parthian
instr.	instrumental
Lat.	Latin
lit.	literally
loc.	locative
m.	masculine
MMP	Manichaean Middle Persian
MP	Middle Persian
MPa	Manichaean Parthian
nom.	nominative
ob.	*obliquus (casus)* / oblique case
OInd.	Old Indic
OIr.	Old Iranian
OP	Old Persian
Opt.	optative
pl.	plural
PN	proper name
pp.	past participle
PrePrPa	Pre-Proto-Parthian
PrPa	Proto-Parthian
rec.	*rectus (casus)* / direct case
ref.	reference
sc.	*scilicet* / it is permmited to know
sg.	singular
Sgd.	Sogdian
Subj.	subjunctive
top.	toponym
ZMP	Zoroastrian Middle Persian
†	ghost word (*corrigendum*)
* / **	reconstructed forms
(...)	letters scarcely readable [in transliterations]
[...]	not readable letters [in transliterations]
°	forms in compound words
?, (?)	doubtful spelling, reading, meaning
!	surprising(ly)

Abbreviations of quoted texts

ANRm	Ardaxšīr I at Naqš-ī-Rustam
AR	Armazi inscriptions

AS	Artabān V at Susa	KSM	Kirdīr at Sar-Mashad (IMP)
AW	Awrōmān parchment	MNFd	Mihr-Narseh at Fīrūzābād (IMP)
BM	Forgery in the silver plaque of the British Museum (ref. to lines of Plate I in MacKenzie 1978)	Nisā	Nisā documents
		NPi	Narseh at Pāikūlī
		SPl	Sar-Pul inscription
		ŠH	Šābuhr I at Hājjīābād
DE	Dura-Europos	ŠKZ	Šābuhr I at the Ka'aba of Zarduxšt
KǰI	Kāl-ī-J̌angāl		
KKZ	Kirdīr at the Ka'aba of Zarduxšt (IMP)	ŠNRb	Šābuhr I at Naqš-ī-Raǰab
KNRb	Kirdīr at Naqš-ī-Raǰab (IMP)	ŠTBq	Šābuhr I at Tang-ī-Borāq
KNRm	Kirdīr at Naqš-ī-Rustam (IMP)	ŠVŠ	Šābuhr I at Weh-Šābuhr

0. INTRODUCTION

0.1. THE FINAL *–y* IN INSCRIPTIONAL MIDDLE PERSIAN AND PARTHIAN

The origin and function of the final *-y* (henceforth -y#) in Inscriptional Middle Persian (IMP) has been a much discussed topic in the history of Iranian Linguistics.[1]

The latest and more exhaustive research on Inscriptional Middle Persian -y# was conducted by Huyse 2003[2]. Huyse 2003, p. 63, proposes the distribution of IMP -y# as follows:

> "(…) ce signe final [i.e., -y#] apparaît toujours après les monosyllabes dans les inscriptions les plus anciennes (…) et après quelques anciens thèmes en -u- (…). *En règle générale*, les di- et polysyllabes présentent un *-y* final après une syllabe à voyelle brève (*ń*^{x} V̌ *y*), mais le *-y* manque dans la plupart des cas après une syllabe à voyelle longue (*n*^{x} V̄́ ø)" (Huyse 2003, p. 63).[3]

A different point of view has more recently been presented by Milizia 2011. Although he admits that -y# probably harks back to an original oblique singular *-ē* (< OIr. **-ahi̯a*) in Inscriptional Middle Persian, and that after the loss of this final (phonological) vowel -y# could have survived as a graphic archaism in the nominal forms, he argues that it was initially interpreted as a final word delimiter, just like the final stroke in Zoroastrian Middle Persian (Milizia 2011, p. 90-91).

His main arguments for this thesis are that IMP -y# occurs not only in the singular nominal inflexion, but also in plural forms, in the verbal conjugation, and in the infinitives (Milizia 2011, p. 69, 90-91). In favor of this assumption, there is the further fact that there are many instances in which the final -y# is ignored because the word is already well delimited (i.e., -y# would be redundant as a word delimiter):

> "(...) l'abbreviatura rappresentata dall'assenza di ⟨-y⟩ è favorita da una circostanza peculiare: infatti, in base ad un semplice principio di economia grafica, ci si attende che un segno di fine di parola possa essere

1 Among others, Meillet 1900, Henning 1958, Windfuhr 1975, Back 1978,

2 Reviewed by Cantera 2006, p. 148-153.

3 The many exceptions to this rule are explained in the same research.

> omesso là dove la posizione della frontiera tra parole sia deducibile da altri elementi, e ciò si verifica sicuramente quando alla fine della parola figuri un morfo che abbia funzione desinenziale o suffissale e frequenza sufficientemente alta da risultare rapidamente riconoscibile; [...] un significante grafico sufficientemente perspicuo" (Milizia 2011, p. 74).

Although the graphic conventions of the -y# writings are something related both in Inscriptional Middle Persian and in Inscriptional Parthian, Milizia's assumption does not apply for Inscriptional Parthian, since -y# does not appear here either in plural forms or in the verbal conjugation. Moreover, it seems to me that it is not suitable for Inscriptional Middle Persian either.[4] If -y# were already a word delimiter in Inscriptional Middle Persian, one would expect it to be always (or almost always) omitted, at least at the end of the line, where a word is never carried over into the next line, since its delimiter function would have been rendered redundant. However, there are numerous instances of it in Inscriptional Middle Persian: ANRm 2 ⟨ctry⟩, ŠNRb 4 and ŠKZ 27 ⟨pʾpky⟩, ŠKZ 14 ⟨[kys]ly⟩, ŠH 11 ⟨ʾwlndly⟩, ŠVŠ 2 and 11 ⟨šhpwhry⟩, ŠVŠ 8 ⟨krty⟩, KNRm 3 ⟨kʾmkʾly⟩, KKZ 2 ⟨gwnk[t](ly)⟩, KNRm 11 ⟨kʾmkʾlytly⟩, KNRm 12 ⟨pʾthštly⟩, KNRm 17 ⟨ʾtwry⟩, KNRm 18 ⟨gty⟩, KKZ 6 ⟨ʾwlwʾhmy⟩, KNRm 19 ⟨[n]pšty⟩, KNRm 20 ⟨g(ʾ)sy⟩, KNRm 21 ⟨š[tl]y⟩, KNRm 27 ⟨štly⟩, KSM 13 ⟨bštyhy⟩, KNRm 30 ⟨gwkʾnyhy⟩, KNRm 31 ⟨ʾpzʾdyhy⟩, KNRm 34 ⟨št(l)y⟩, KNRm 36 ⟨ʾtwry⟩, etc. Instances appear even in IPa, e.g., ŠKZ 1 ⟨ʾrmny⟩, ŠKZ 4 ⟨bybʾlšy⟩, ŠKZ 8, 13 ⟨hmkwsy⟩, ŠKZ 22 ⟨nywdpty⟩, ŠH 11 ⟨pty⟩, ŠH 13 ⟨šyty⟩).

Furthermore, we can assume that -y# is used in such instances to fill the line, but this is unlikely, e.g. ŠKZ 27 ⟨pʾpky⟩ (see Fig. I), where -y# is effectively reduced (cf. the end of this line with the previous one ⟨BREr⟩ [see Fig. II], with an empty space after the word). This latter consideration is also applicable to Inscriptional Parthian: ŠKZ 4 ⟨bybʾlšy⟩ (see Fig. III), ŠKZ 8 ⟨hmkwsy⟩ (see Fig. IV), ŠKZ 13 ⟨hmkwsy⟩ (see Fig. V).

In addition, if -y# was interpreted fairly early on as a word delimiter, it is not easy to understand why it does not appear after the Aramaeograms. According to Milizia's opinion (Milizia 2011, p. 90):

> "(...) per il fatto di non figurare nelle parole eterografiche, il segno ⟨y⟩ finale acquisisce potenzialmente, accanto a quella di delimitatore grafico, la funzione di diacritico segnalatore di scrittura non aramaica".

---

4 See 3.2.3.3 and 4.4.2.2 for my explanations of the absence of -y# in some Inscriptional Parthian suffixal forms.

In fact, this assumption implies that -y# was already considered in Inscriptional Middle Persian more as a phonographic element (hardly related to its origin) than as a simple word delimiter (cf. the final stroke in Zoroastrian Middle Persian, which often appears in Aramaeographic forms).

As Huyse 2003 did for Inscriptional Middle Persian, I have also accepted a phonological explanation of the presence or absence of -y# for Inscriptional Parthian in this paper.

0.2. THE ORIGIN OF THE FINAL *–y*

The most extended opinion is that the -y# harks back to the Old Iranian oblique ending (**-ahi̯a* or others). The study by Back 1978 is an exception, for he did not recognize a case-system in Middle Persian. Huyse 2003, p. 58 ff., has pointed out, however, that Inscriptional Middle Persian (Skjærvø 1983a), Manichaean Middle Persian (Sims-Williams 1981) and the Pahlavi Translation of the Avesta (Cantera 1999) reveal traces of a system in which the direct and oblique cases were formally and functionally distinct.

For Huyse, the origin of this -y# could not only be the old thematic genitive singular, but also any one of the following cases: loc. sg.m. of -a- stems, OP *-ay-ā*; gen./abl./loc./instr. sg.f. of -ā- stems, OP *-āyā*^{h}; abl./loc. sg.m./f. of -ī̆- stems, OP *-iyā*^{h} (*apud* Huyse 2003, p. 73). The -y# could have had an ancient value *-ē̆*$^{(h)}$ (for Huyse 2003, p. 96) or *-ə* (for Back 1978, p. 39), but it was nonetheless purely graphic and without any phonetic value, at least from the 3rd-4th centuries onward, as confirmed by Manichaean Middle Persian (MMP) and Manichaean Parthian (MPa), where -y# simply does not occur (Henning 1958, p. 64 ff.).[5]

0.3. FINAL *–y* IN INSCRIPTIONAL PARTHIAN: STATE OF THE ART

Although -y# also appears in Inscriptional Parthian (IPa) and the issues concerning the function and distribution of Inscriptional Middle Persian -y# have prompted an intense debate, the Parthian -y# has been given very little attention, and no distribution has been proposed for it.

Ghilain 1939, p. 13, when referring to the Parthian versions of the great

---

5 I am unable to prove whether this -y# did or did not have a phonetic value in the earliest Parthian (non-Manichaean) documents. It has been accepted that this sign still represents a linguistic reality in the documents of Nisā (ref. in Durkin-Meisterernst 2014, p. 112). This does not, however, fall within the scope of this paper.

Sassanian inscriptions, stated that "(…) un bon nombre de graphies restent traditionnelles et archaïques, par exemple celles qui maintiennent les voyelles finales (…)".

Sixty-four years later, and when dealing with the Inscriptional Middle Persian compounds in ⟨-pt(y)⟩[6], Huyse comments that Inscriptional Parthian, unlike Middle Persian, generally has -y# in this kind of compound, and he argues:

> "Le *y* final parthe est apparemment soumis à d'autres règles qu'en moyen-perse, sans qu'on puisse établir de véritable justification pour sa présence ou son absence.[7] Mais comme le (moyen-)parthe est une langue fort conservatrice et archaïsante, il 'simule' de temps à autre des formes vieil-iraniennes qui en réalité étaient prononcées 'à la moderne', comme le démontre la comparaison avec les textes parthes manichéens (cf. Henning 1958, 64sq.)" (Huyse 2003, p. 37-38, fn. 38).

This paper provides an overview of the use and distribution of -y# in Inscriptional Parthian. I have used the term "Inscriptional Parthian" (IPa) for all non-Manichaean Parthian (MPa) sources: inscriptions, parchments and the documents of Nisā. The Inscriptional Parthian vocabulary of Gignoux 1972a has been used as the basic reference, having revised it and checked the entries against the original and later editions and facsimiles of the original texts.[8] I have followed the system of references to sources and

---

6 Compounds in ⟨-pt(y)⟩ do not have the -y# in Inscriptional Middle Persian, except for ŠKZ 32 ⟨dzpty⟩, ŠKZ 34 ⟨dlpty⟩, NPi 31 F5,02 ⟨dyhpty⟩, NPi 45 H2,04 ⟨nhwpty⟩. The -y# is not readable in NPi 16 C2,05 ⟨mgw(pt)[y]⟩.

7 My own emphasis.

8 Main consulted editions and facsimiles (for references to works before 1972, s. Gignoux 1972a, p. 43-44, and p. 9-14 for those inscriptions containing a Middle Persian version) are the following: 1) for the inscription of Ardaxšīr I at Naqš-ī-Rustam (ANRm), Back 1978, p. 281-282; 2) for the Armazi inscriptions (AR), Henning 1961 (not reported in Gignoux's vocabulary); 3) for the Awrōmān parchment, Minns 1915 and Cowley 1919 (with Plates; see Plate IV in this work taken from Minns), see also Nyberg 1923 and MacKenzie 1985, and the recent edition in Skjærvø 1995, p. 290; 4) for the forgery in a silver plaque of the British Museum containing the text of Šābuhr's shooting (BM), MacKenzie 1978 [rpt. 1999], with plate and facsimil; 5) for Dura-Europos, plates I-XXXIV in Frye 1968, and see also Perkins 1959; 6) for the Kāl-ī-J̌angāl inscription, see Plate V in this work, taken from Henning 1953; 7) for Nisā documents, Diakonoff/Livshits 1977-1999; 8) for the inscription of Narseh at Pāikūlī (NPi), Humbach 1978, Skjærvø/Humbach 1980, Skjærvø 1983b, 1983c, and Cereti/Terribili 2014; 9) for the inscription of Šābuhr I at Hāǰǰīābād (ŠH) and at Tang-ī-Borāq (ŠTBq), Back 1978, p. 372-378, and MacKenzie 1978

passages in Gignoux's vocabulary, except for texts which he did not use and for the inscription of Narseh in Pāikūlī, where the references have been made according to the synoptic tables presented by Humbach/Skjærvø 1980 and the edition and glossary provided by Skjærvø 1983b, together with the new identificated blocks recently published by Cereti/Terribili 2014, indicating the number of the line, the block number (in small letters for the Parthian version and in capital letters for the Middle Persian one) and the line of the block, e.g., NPi 2 a11,02: Narseh at Pāikūlī, line 2 of the Parthian version, block a11, line 2 of the block. I have used a footnote whenever my reading of a word differs from Gignoux.

This is a preliminary study in which I have considered mainly the basic Inscriptional Parthian vocabulary: common nouns (substantives and adjectives), verbs, adverbs, conjunctions, prepositions and particles. The use of -y# in anthroponyms, theonyms, toponyms, names of wines, and compounds with a first element ending in ⟨-y⟩ still awaits an exhaustive classification and study.

[rpt. 1999], the reproduction of this inscription in the bowl in Yale is edited by Skjærvø 1990, p. 290-291, see Plate III in this work, and a concordance of the Middle Persian and Parthian versions, including the forgery of the British Museum silver plaque, in Ferrer-Losilla 2013; 10) for the inscription of Šābuhr I at the Ka'aba of Zarduxšt (ŠKZ), Back 1978, p. 284-372, and Huyse 1999; 11) for the inscription of Šābuhr I at Naqš-ī-Rağab (ŠNRb), Back 1978, p. 282-284; 12) for the inscription of Šābuhr I at Weh-Šābuhr (ŠVŠ), Back 1978, p. 378-383. For the Middle Persian incriptions of Mihr-Narseh at Fīrūzābād (MNFd), Back 1978, p. 498; and for the incriptions of Kirdīr (at the Ka'aba of Zarduxšt [KKZ], at Naqš-ī-Rağab [KNRb], at Naqš-ī-Rustam [KNRm] and at Sar-Mashad [KSM]), Gignoux 1972b, p. 177-205, Brunner 1974, p. 97-113, Back 1978, p. 384-489, Gignoux 1991, and the last concordance in Jügel 2010.

1. ARAMAEOGRAMS AND PHONOGRAPHIC COMPLEMENTS

1.1. ARAMAEOGRAMS

The first clear statement is that -y# does not appear in the Inscriptional Parthian Aramaeograms.[9] When -y# appears, it is always part of the Aramaeogram:

a) ⟨AYTY⟩ *ast* "he is" (MPa ⟨ʾst, ʾsṯ⟩). Notice that together with ⟨AYTY⟩ (NPi 24 d3,06, 30 e3,06, 39 g10,03, Nisā 211/3, 658/6, 798/6, 1379/8, N. 210/6), ⟨AYT⟩ also occurs (Nisā 447/2, 556/2, 661/2, 676/2, 1409/3);

b) ⟨LY⟩ *man* "to me" ŠH 1, ŠKZ 30, ŠTBq 1 (MPa ⟨mn⟩). Inscriptional Parthian ⟨LY⟩ is actually the Aramaic preposition *l-* "to/for" plus the 1st sg. L-Set oblique suffixe *-i* "me", cf. Hoberman 1988, p. 562, about the different nominal and L-Set suffixes in some Aramaic dialects. This assumption was also defended by Basharin 2011.[10]

The following Aramaeograms also have an ending ⟨-Y⟩, which is probably the reflex of the Aramaic suffix *-y*:[11]

c) ⟨AHY⟩ (cf. Aram. ⟨ʾḥ⟩) *brād* "brother" Nisā 54/1 *et passim*, AW 3 (MPa ⟨brʾd⟩);

d) ⟨AMY⟩ (cf. Aram. ⟨ʾm⟩) *mād* "mother" ŠKZ 21, 23 (MPa ⟨mʾd⟩);

e) ⟨BRY⟩ (cf. Aram. ⟨br⟩ [⟨br-h⟩]) *puhr* "son" Nisā 1760/1, 2, AW 1, 3, 5, 6, AS 2, AR 5, ANRm 3, NPi 1 a5,01 (⟨BR[Y]⟩), ŠH 3, ŠKZ 1, 18, 19, 21, 30, ŠNRb 2, ŠTBq 2, ŠVŠ 6, BM 3, 17 (MPa ⟨pwhr⟩, IPa ⟨BRY LBRY⟩ *puhr^{e}puhr*[12] "grandson" ŠKZ 1, ŠNRb 4);

---

9 The Aramaeograms do not have a final -y# either in Inscriptional Middle Persian.

10 I want to thank Pavel Basharin, who kindly sent me his handout.

11 Basharin 2011 has pointed out that ⟨Y⟩ (in forms like IPa/IMP ⟨AHY⟩, IPa/IMP ⟨AMY⟩, IPa ⟨BRY⟩ [and ⟨BRY LBRY⟩] and IPa ⟨BRTY⟩) is probably not the Aramaic constructus m.pl. *y*, but the Aramaic suffix *-y* which sometimes appears, although not read, in nouns in some Aramaic dialects. Henning 1958, p. 34, however, considered that the Aramaic (possessive) form for "mein Brüder" (*ʾḥy*) is the basis for IPa/IMP ⟨AHY⟩, but see also Bailey 1943, p. 2, who considered that the -y# was probably the "oblique case of Middle Persian, rather than the Aramaic pronoun of the first person, 'my' (...)".

12 When a vowel is transcribed above, I indicate that there is no certainty whether

f) ⟨BRTY⟩ (cf. Aram. ⟨brt⟩ [⟨brt-h⟩]) *duxt* "daughter" AR 1, ŠKZ 1, 18, 21, 22 (MPa ⟨dwxt⟩).
g) In the case of ⟨ZY⟩ *čē*, a linking particle-*iẓāfat* (Nisā *passim*, AW 2, AS 4, NPi *passim*, AR *passim*; MPa ⟨cy, t̠šy⟩), ⟨ZY⟩ may be the Inscriptional Parthian representation of Old Aramaic *zy*.[13]

1.2. PHONOGRAPHIC COMPLEMENTS

The final -y# does not usually appear in the phonographic complements attached to some Aramaeograms in the verbal forms or in the nominal morphology.

Following list shows the phonographic complements which appear in the verbal Aramaeograms:[14]

- ***Ind. 1sg.*** ⟨HWYm⟩ *(a)hēm* "I am" ŠKZ 1 (MPa ⟨ʾhym, hym⟩); ⟨H[HSN]Wm⟩ *dārām* "I have" ŠKZ 1 (MPa ⟨dʾrʾm⟩); ⟨OBDWm⟩ *karām* "I make" ŠKZ 2, NPi 27 e6,03 (MPa ⟨krʾm⟩);
- ***Ind. 1pl.*** ⟨HHSNWm⟩ *dārām* "we have" ŠKZ 17 (MPa ⟨dʾrʾm⟩); ⟨HZYWm⟩ *wēnām* "we see" NPi 8 b5,02 (MPa ⟨wynʾm⟩); ⟨KTŠWm⟩ *kōšām*[(?)] "we fight" NPi 27 e5,03; ⟨ŠLHWm⟩ *frašāwām* "we send" NPi 22 d1,04, 27 e13,03, 38 g4,02; ⟨YBOEm⟩ *wxāzām* "we ask for" ŠKZ 17 (MPa ⟨wxʾzʾm⟩); ⟨YDOEm⟩ *zānām* "we know" NPi 39 g7,03 (MPa ⟨zʾnʾm⟩); ⟨YΘYBWm⟩ *nišīdām*[15] "we sit (we set down)" ŠKZ 17 (cf. MPa 3sg. ⟨nšydyd⟩); ⟨YNTNm⟩ *dahām* "we give" ŠKZ 19 (MPa 1sg. ⟨dhʾm⟩); ⟨HWYm⟩ *(a)hēm*[(?)] "we are" ŠKZ 3, 4, 9, 29; NPi 20 d3,02 (≠ MPa Ind. 1pl. ⟨hymʾd⟩); ⟨[Y](HWEm)⟩[16] *bawām* "we become" NPi 19 d13,01 (MPa ⟨bwʾm⟩); ⟨YMΘAEm⟩ *rasām*[17]

---

it has a phonetic value. Cf. the phonographic writing ⟨pwhrypwhr⟩ in ŠH 4 and ŠTBq 3.

13 This particle is analyzed as an original (semitic) genitive sigular masculine pronoun, which was yet a relative particle in Old Aramaic (Pat-El 2008, p. 57-58).

14 For a discussion of the grammatical verbal categories, see Ferrer-Losilla 2013, p. 179-203.

15 Gignoux 1972a, p. 67: †⟨YDRYKWm⟩.

16 Gignoux 1972a, p. 53: †⟨HWEm⟩; cf. Humbach/Skjærvø 1980 ⟨[](HWEm)⟩, and NPi 21 D10,04 ⟨(YHWWN)[m]⟩ in the Inscriptional Middle Persian version.

17 Probable reading. The Aramaeogram IPa ⟨YMΘAE-⟩ appears in the Inscriptional Middle Persian version of Narseh at Pāikūlī as ⟨YHMTWN-⟩

"we arrive" NPi 13 c11,01;

- ***Ind.***[18] ***3sg.*** ⟨hyp ATYEt⟩ *hēb āsēd* "may he come" NPi 17 c2,05 (MPa ⟨ʾsyd, ʾsyyd⟩); ⟨YCBEt⟩ *kāmēd* "he wants" NPi 3 a6,03 (MPa ⟨kʾmyd, qʾmyd⟩); ⟨YDOEt⟩ *zānēd* "he knows" NPi 23 d15,05, 26 e5,02 (MPa ⟨zʾnyd⟩); ⟨hyp YMLLWt⟩ *hēb wāčēd* "he should say" NPi 30 e12,06, 33 f13,03 (MPa ⟨wʾcyd⟩); ⟨HQAYMWt⟩[19] *awĕštēd* "he stands/places" NPi 5 a13-14,05, 13 c12,03, 20 d11,02 (cf. MPa ⟨ʿyštyd, ʿštyd⟩); ⟨hyp HQAMWd⟩ *hēb awĕstēd* "may he place" ŠH 12; ⟨YBOEd⟩ *wxāzēd* "he wants" NPi 16 c14,04 (MPa ⟨wxʾzyd⟩); ⟨YHWEd⟩ *bawēd* "he becomes" NPi 18 c14-15,06 (MPa ⟨bwyd⟩);
- ***Ind. 3pl.*** ⟨ATYEnt⟩ *āsēnd* "they come" NPi 43 g16,07, 21 d13-14,03 (MPa ⟨ʾsynd⟩); ⟨OBDWnt⟩ *karēnd* "they make" ŠKZ 17, NPi 4 a7,04 (MPa ⟨krynd, qrynd⟩); ⟨HQAYMWnt⟩ *ĕštēnd* "they stand" NPi 9 b9,03, 40 g16,04, ŠKZ 22 (MPa ⟨ʿštynd, ʿyštyynd⟩); ⟨HHSNWnt⟩ *dārēnd* "they have" NPi 13 c3,01 (MPa ⟨dʾrynd⟩); ⟨ŠLHWnt⟩ *frašāwēnd* "they send" NPi 21 d15,03 (MPa ⟨fršʾwynd⟩); ⟨AŠMOYWnt⟩ *ašnawēnd* "they understand" NPi 16 c3,04 (MPa ⟨ʾšnwynd⟩); ⟨YHWEnt⟩ *bawēnd* "they become" NPi 15 c10-11,03 (MPa ⟨bwynd⟩); ⟨AŠTYWnt⟩ *wxarēnd* "they eat" NPi 11 b15,05 (cf. MPa ⟨ʾxwrynd, ʾwxrynd⟩); ⟨HWE(nt)⟩ *(a)hēnd* NPi 7 b4,01 (MPa ⟨ʾhynd, ʾʾhyynd⟩); ⟨HWEnt⟩ **ahānd* NPi 6 a14,06 (Impf.?, cf. Impf. 3sg. MPa ⟨ʾhʾz⟩)[20];
- ***Ind. 2pl.*** ⟨OBDWt⟩ *karēd* "you make" NPi 34 f13,04 (MPa ⟨kryd, qryd⟩); ⟨HWEd⟩ *(a)hēd* "you are" NPi 40 g6,04, 22 d11,04 (MPa ⟨hyd, ʾhyd⟩); ⟨HWYt⟩ *(a)hēd* NPi 39 g16,03;

(=ZMP), which corresponds with Manichaean Middle Persian ⟨rs-⟩, e.g., 3sg. ind. ⟨rsyd, rsyyd⟩, 3sg. subj. ⟨rsʾd⟩.

18 When the particle ⟨hyp⟩ occurs, the form is to be considered an optative.

19 ⟨HQAYMW-⟩ is used in Inscriptional Parthian in the transitive ("to place") or intransitive ("to stand"). In Manichaean Parthian the transitive form is *awĕst-* (MPa ⟨ʾwyst-, ʾwst-⟩), while the intransitive one is *ĕšt-* (MPa ⟨ʿyšt-, ʿšt-⟩). Together with these, we also find MPa ⟨ʾwyšt-, ʾwšt-⟩ *awĕšt-*, in both the transitive and intransitive. Cf. Skjærvø 1983c, p. 22-23 (fn. 7): "(...) [sc. ⟨HQAYMW-⟩] represents both the transitive verb Pa *awestādan* 'to place' (Ghilain 90) and the intransitive one *(aw)ištādan* 'to stand, to place oneself' (Ghilain 78-79)."

20 For the imperfect of *(a)h-*, see Ferrer-Losilla 2013, p. 453 ff., with bibliography.

- ***Impv. 2pl.*** ⟨YHWEd⟩[21] *bawēd* "be (you)" NPi 40 g9,04 (MPa ⟨bwyd⟩); ⟨HQ[AY]MWt⟩ *(aw)ēštēd* "place (you)" NPi 37 g9-10,01 (MPa ⟨ʾwystyd⟩);
- ***Subj. 1sg.*** ⟨OBDWn⟩ *karān* "I will make" NPi 3 a14,03 (MPa ⟨krʾn⟩); ⟨YDOEn⟩ *zānān* "I will know" NPi 11b8,05 (cf. MPa Subj. 1pl. ⟨zʾnʾm⟩); ⟨YNTNWn⟩ *dahān* "I will give" NPi 3 a11,03, 17 c7,05 (MPa ⟨dhʾn⟩);
- ***Subj. 1pl.*** ⟨OBDWm⟩ *karām* "we will make" NPi 5 a11,05, 17 c15,05 (MPa ⟨krʾm, qrʾm⟩);
- ***Subj. 3sg.*** ⟨YDOEd⟩ *zānāδ* "he will know" ŠKZ 17 (cf. MPa ⟨zʾnʾ, zʾnʾ(h̲)⟩); ⟨OBDWd⟩ *karāδ* "he will make" NPi 10 b8,04, 24 d15,06 (cf. MPa ⟨krʾ, krʾh̲⟩); ⟨ŠLHWd⟩ *frašāwāδ* "he will send" NPi 10 b7,04 (cf. MPa ⟨fršʾwʾ, fršʾwʾh̲⟩); ⟨ŠBQWd⟩ *hirzāδ* "hi will let" NPi 10 b2,04 (cf. MPa ⟨hyrzʾh̲⟩); ⟨HQAYMWd⟩ *ēštāδ* "he will stand" NPi 33 f3,03, 35 f7,05 (cf. MPa ⟨ʿyštʾh̲, ʿštʾh̲⟩); ⟨[HQA]YMWt⟩ *ēštāδ* NPi 5 a14,05; ⟨HWYt⟩ *ahād* NPi 3 a17,03, 37 g2,01, 4 a11,04, 5 a11,05, 34 f2,04, 36 f6,06, 19 d15,01, ŠKZ 29 (MPa ⟨ʾhʾd⟩); ⟨YMΘAEt⟩ *rasāδ* (?) "he will arrive" NPi 35 f13,05 (see fn. 17);
- ***Subj. 3pl.*** ⟨AŠMOYWnt⟩ *išnawānd* "they will listen" NPi 8 b15,02,[22] 20 d1,02 (cf. MPa Ind. 3pl. ⟨ʿšnwynd⟩); ⟨YHWEnt⟩ *bawānd* "they will be" NPi 31 f14,01 (cf. MPa Ind. 3pl. ⟨bwynd⟩); ⟨YHYEnt⟩ *bawānd* ŠKZ 30; ⟨OBDWnt⟩ *karānd* "they will make" ŠKZ 30 (cf. MPa Ind. 3pl. ⟨krynd, qrynd⟩); ⟨HWYEnt⟩ *ahānd* NPi 16 c2,04 (cf. MPa Subj. 3sg. ⟨ʾhʾd⟩); ⟨HWYNt⟩ *ahānd* ŠH 11, ŠTBq 5, BM 11;
- ***Subj. 2pl.*** ⟨AŠMOYWd⟩ *išnawād* "you will listen" NPi 11 b7,05 (cf. MPa Subj. 3sg. ⟨ʿšnwʾh̲⟩);
- ***Past participles***[23] ⟨AHDt⟩ *grift* "taken" NPi 7 a17,06 [⟨AH(D)t⟩], 26 e6,02 (MPa ⟨gryft⟩); ⟨ASRt⟩ *bast* "bound" NPi 26 e6,02, 2 a11,02 [⟨(A)SRt⟩] (MPa ⟨bst⟩); ⟨ATYt⟩ *āgad* "come" NPi 7 b7,01, 15 c9,03

---

[21] Gignoux 1972a, p. 67: †⟨YHWEm⟩. For the transliteration ⟨YHWEd⟩, see Humbach 1978, p. 28: "⟨šʾt YHWEd⟩. Edd. ⟨šʾt YHWEm⟩ Hf2. ⟨šʾty HWEd⟩ Frye."

[22] Gignoux 1972a, p. 47: †⟨AŠMOYWnm⟩ *ašnawēnām* ? (*sic*) "j'annonce". Gignoux's transcription was taken from Herzfeld 1924, although the new transliterations of the latter had offered yet another reading ⟨AŠMOYWnt⟩ (*apud* Humbach 1978, p. 26). Skjærvø 1983b, p. 36 and 88: Ind. 3pl.

[23] Since past participles with a phonographic complement ⟨-t⟩ are very numerous, only a few instances have been reported here.

[⟨A(TYt)⟩], ŠKZ 3 [⟨AT[Y]t⟩], 4, 9, Nisā N.105/1 (MPa ⟨ʾgd, ʾʾgd⟩); ⟨OBDt⟩ *kird* "made" ŠKZ 3, 4 (2x), 5, 11 (2x), 12, 16, 17 (2x), 29, NPi 1 a14,01, 13 c12,01, 29 e13,05, 36 f13,06, 3 a16,03, 32 f2,02, 15 c11,03, Nisā 867/3 (MPa ⟨kyrd, qyrd⟩); ⟨QΘLt⟩ *ōžad* "killed" ŠKZ 4, 5 (MPa ⟨ʾwjd⟩); ⟨YHWt⟩ *būd* "been" ŠKZ 16 and *passim* (MPa ⟨bwd⟩); ⟨YBOt⟩ *wxāšt* "asked for" ŠKZ 29 (MPa ⟨wxʾšt⟩); ⟨BNYt⟩ *dišt* "built" ŠH 9, 11 (MPa ⟨dyšt⟩); ⟨HHSNt⟩ *dird* "had" ŠKZ 25,29 (MPa ⟨dyrd⟩); ⟨HQAYMWt⟩ *(aw)ištād* "stood" ŠKZ 3, 4, 19, ŠH 7, BM 7 (MPa ⟨ʿyštʾd, ʿštʾd, ʾwyštʾd, ʾwštʾd⟩); ⟨HWBDWt⟩ *wigand*[24] "destroyed" ŠKZ 4 (MPa ⟨wygnd⟩); ⟨HZYt⟩ *dīd* "seen" NPi 23 d1,05 (MPa ⟨dyd⟩); ⟨KTYBt⟩ *nibišt* "written" ŠKZ 16, 19, 22 (MPa ⟨nbyšt⟩); ⟨RMYt⟩ *abgand* "thrown" ŠH 7, ŠTBq 5, BM 7 (MPa ⟨ʾbgnd⟩); ⟨ŠDYt⟩ *wist* "thrown" ŠH 5, 6, ŠTBq 3, 4, BM 5, 6 (= IMP); ⟨YMΘAt⟩ *rasīd*? "arrived" NPi 20 d3,02 (see fn. 17);

- ***Infinitives*** ⟨HQAYMtn⟩ *(aw)ištādan* "to stand" NPi 3 a7,03 (cf. MPa ppp. ⟨ʿyštʾd, ʾwštʾd⟩); ⟨OBDtn⟩ *kirdan* "to make" NPi 11 b5,05, 17 c14,05 (MPa ⟨kyrdn, qyrdn⟩); ⟨YNTNtn⟩ *dādan* "to give" NPi 4 a13,04 [⟨YN(T)Ntn⟩], 38 g16,02 (MPa ⟨dʾdn⟩); ⟨HHSNtn⟩ *dirdan* "to have" NPi 34 f2,04, 31 f6,01 [⟨HHS(Nt)[n]⟩] (MPa ⟨dyrdn⟩); ⟨KTYBtn⟩ *nibištan* "to write" ŠKZ 16 (MPa ⟨nbyštn⟩); ⟨YOBDytn⟩ *yazīdan*?? "to sacrifice" (cf. IMP ŠKZ 27 ⟨YDBHWNtn⟩ *yaštan*).

Other phonographic complements occur outside the verbal morphology: ⟨ABYtr⟩ *pidar* (MPa ⟨pydr⟩) "by/to the father" (ŠKZ 16, NPi 37 g9,01), ⟨BRBYTAn⟩ *wispuhrān* (MPa ⟨wyspwhrʾʾn⟩) ob.pl. "princes" (ŠH 6, ŠTBq 4, BM 6, 20, NPi 2 a14,02, 7 b5,01, 37 g16,01, 39 g2,03, 39 g9,03), ⟨LHw⟩ *hō/haw* (MPa ⟨hw⟩) "he" (ŠKZ 5, ŠH 7, NPi 2 a11,02 and *passim*), ⟨LHwp⟩ *hō-b* "he, certainly" (ŠH 14, ŠTBq 6, BM 14), ⟨LHwyn⟩ *hawīn* (MPa ⟨hwyn⟩) "they" (ŠKZ 22, NPi 12 b10,06 [⟨(LHwyn)⟩], 28 e6,04, 29 e5,05, 32 f8,02), ⟨OBDk⟩ *bandag* (MPa ⟨bndg⟩; cf. IMP ⟨OBDky⟩) "servant" (NPi 5 a12,05, 6 a12,06), ⟨PNEstr⟩ *awaristar* (cf. MPa ⟨ʾwr⟩) "further down" (ŠH 10, BM 10-11 [⟨PNE/st^{r}⟩]).

A final -y# occurs in the phonographic complement of the optative form ⟨HWYndy⟩ *ahēndē* "he may be": ⟨šʾYWt HWYndy⟩ *šahād*? *ahēndē*$^{(h)}$ "he would have been able" (NPi 32 f3,02), ⟨BNYt HWYndy⟩ *dišt ahēndē*$^{(h)}$ "he would have built" (ŠH 9, BM 9), ⟨YHWt HWYndy⟩ *būd ahēndē*$^{(h)}$ "he would have been" (ŠH 9-10, BM 10), ⟨HWYndy⟩ *ahēndē*$^{(h)}$ "he would be"

24 Huyse 1999, Band 1, p. 26, transcribes **wānād* "vernichtet".

(NPi 33 f7,03, 35 f6,05). But in these instances, ⟨-y⟩ is obviously the spelling of the final *-ē* of the optative ending, MPa ⟨ʾhyndy, ʾhyndyh̲, ʾhyndyy, ʾhyndyyh̲⟩ *ahēndē* (cf. Bact. enclitic 3pl. Opt. -ινδηιο [and variants]; Henning 1960, p. 54 [fn. 8], Sims-Williams 2007, p. 42-43).

The only real Aramaeograms with a phonographic complement ending in -y# are the abstract nouns in ⟨-py⟩ *-ī̆f* (MPa *-ī̆ft*, MP *-īh*): ⟨OBDkpy⟩[25] *bandagī̆f* "servitude, bondage" (ŠKZ 3) and ⟨ΘBpy⟩ *nēwī̆f* "courage" (ŠKZ 16, 17, 29), which show the -y# as they do in the phonographic forms. This ending will be discussed below within the Inscriptional Parthian phonographic forms ending in ⟨-(y)py⟩ (see 3.2.3.4).

---

25 ŠKZ 3 ⟨OBDkpy⟩. The reconstruction †⟨OB[Dkpy]]⟩ by Skjærvø 1983b, p. 51, in NPi 22 d11-12,04 must be corrected by ⟨RB[A]⟩ (Cereti/Terribili 2014, p. 369).

2. PHONOGRAPHIC FORMS: NOUNS ENDING IN A VOWEL AND NOUNS OUTSIDE THE NOMINAL INFLECTION

2.1. WORDS ENDING IN A FINAL LONG VOWEL OR A GLIDE

In phonographic forms, an ending in ⟨-y⟩ is sometimes used to indicate the ending in a (long) vowel or a glide.[26] Since this ⟨-y⟩ had a phonetic value, or was used to indicate a word-final long vowel, there is not *sensu stricto* a final -y#[27] in such instances, e.g.: ⟨ʾpwmʾy⟩ (ŠKZ 6) **Apōmiyā* (Apameia, top.), ⟨ʾšʾy⟩ (DE 4,1) *Ašā* (Aša, m. PN), ⟨ʾwrhʾy⟩ (ŠKZ 9, 11) *Urhā* (Edessa, top.), ⟨ʾwrnʾy⟩ (ŠKZ 6) *Urnā* (Urima, top.), ⟨ʾygʾy⟩ (ŠKZ 12) *Aygā* (Aigaia, top.), ⟨ʾypynʾy⟩ (ŠKZ 13) *Ēpī(fa)n(iy)ā* (Epiphaneia, top.), ⟨dwlʾy⟩ (ŠKZ 7) *Dūrā* (Dura, top.), ⟨glʾtynʾy⟩ (ŠKZ 10) *Galātīniyā* (Galatia, top.), ⟨knšrʾy⟩ (ŠKZ 6) **Kinašrā* (Khalcis, top.), ⟨krtrʾy⟩ (ŠKZ 12) **Katabalā* (Katabolos, top.), ⟨kstʾprʾy⟩ (ŠKZ 13) *Kastābalā* (Kastabala, top.), ⟨(s)wrʾy⟩ (ŠKZ 5) *Sūrā* (Sura, top.), ⟨twdynʾy⟩ (ŠKZ 14) *Tūyanā* (Tyana, top.), ⟨hmpy⟩ (Nisā 62/2, 631/3, 1230/3, 1436/2, 1512/2, 1740/2, 2027/2, 2156/3) *Hampī* (?, top.), ⟨ʾphwny⟩ (Nisā N. 280a/3, 280b/3) *Apāxunī* (name of a day), ⟨hwmy⟩ (Nisā 722/7) *Humāy* (top.), ⟨ʾbyny⟩ (DE 6) *Abinnay* (?, PN), ⟨mtrpry⟩ (AW 6) *Mihrfriy* (PN), ⟨wpry⟩ (Nisā N. 280a/1, 280a/2, 280a/6) *Wifray* (PN).

All these forms are toponyms or proper names. An exception is the common noun ⟨hwtwy⟩ "lord" (ŠKZ 1 [⟨hwt(w)y⟩], 20, 23, 26, NPi 10 b5,04, 21 d4,03, 28 e4,04, 42 g6,06 [⟨h[wt]wy⟩], 42 g9,06, 42 g10,06, 42 g15,06 [⟨h[w]twy⟩], 42 g16,06) and its compound ⟨ktkhwtwy⟩ "lord of the house" (NPi 15 c2,03, 27 e10,03).

Two alternative explanations are possible for this word, and none of them implies a -y# *sensu stricto*. The -y# of IPa ⟨hwtwy⟩ could reflect a Middle Persian loanword. The ancient group OIr. **-āu̯V-* becomes MP *-āy* and Pa *-āw* (e.g. ZMP ⟨dʾlʾy⟩ *dārā(y)* and MPa ⟨dʾrʾw⟩ *dārāw* and ⟨dʾryʾw⟩ *dāryāw*, from OIr. **dārai̯āu̯ahu-* < IIr. **d^hārai̯a-* + **h_1u̯asu-*)[28]. The spelling of Inscriptional Parthian ⟨(°)hwtwy⟩ could perhaps be read **xwadāw* (<

[26] See Huyse 2003, p. 82 ff., for the historical evolution of nouns ending in a long vowel in Middle Persian.

[27] Gignoux 1972a, p. 45: †⟨grmʾny⟩, to be transliterated ⟨grmʾnyʾ⟩, cf. Huyse 1999, Band 1, p. 25-26.

[28] Cf. Werba 1982, p. 148, and Hübschmann 1895, p. 167.

OIr. *hu̯atāu̯a-), but the spellings of Manichean Parthian ⟨xwdʾy⟩ *xwadāy* and ⟨qdyxwdʾy⟩ *kadexwadāy* suggest this word was a Middle Persian loanword in (Manichaean) Parthian, instead of the expected MPa *⟨wxtʾw⟩ **wxadāw*. Accordingly, IPa ⟨hwtwy⟩ and ⟨ktkhwtwy⟩ would be pseudo-historical spellings of *xwadāy* and *kadagxwadāy/ kadexwadāy*.

Another possible explanation is that IPa ⟨(°)hwtwy⟩ is to be read as °*xwadā* (despite MPa ⟨xwdʾy⟩), being ⟨w⟩ a historical spelling of an old **xwadāw*, and the final ⟨y⟩ an indicator for the *-ā#*.

2.2. NOUNS OUTSIDE THE NOMINAL INFLECTION

Since -y# is supposed to hark back to an ancient case of the nominal inflexion (probably a singular oblique case, as I have briefly summarized in 0.2), Inscriptional Parthian -y# is expected to appear only in nominal forms. Hence, the following groups of words never have -y#: uninflected words (2.2.1) and verbal inflectional forms and infinitives (2.2.2).

2.2.1. Uninflected words

Inscriptional Parthian uninflected forms, that is to say, adverbs, conjunctions, prepositions and particles, do not have the -y#: ⟨ʾkm⟩ *āgām* "or"[29] NPi 33 f7,03, 39 g7,03, 39 g9,03 (MPa ⟨ʾgʾm⟩); ⟨ʾdyn⟩ *adyān* ŠH 10, BM 10, NPi 3 a17,03, 7 b4,02, 9 b12,03, 28 e10,04, 35 f12,05, 35 f14,05 "then", with intensive suffix IPa ⟨ʾdynš⟩ *adyān-iž* NPi 17 c4,05, 32 f3,02 (MPa ⟨ʾdyʾn, ʾdyʾʾn⟩); ⟨ʾk⟩ *ag* "if" ŠH9, BM 9, NPi 9 b9,03, 11 b10,05, 11 b15,05, 17 c3,05, 28 e6,04, 29 e5,05, 31 f14,01, 33 f3,03, 34 f13,04, 39 g7,03 (MPa ⟨ʾg⟩); ⟨ʾpr⟩ *abar* "on" ŠKZ 3, 5, 9, 19, 22, 23, 24, NPi 3 a7,03, 18 c3,06, 25 e10,01 (MPa ⟨ʾbr⟩); ⟨ʾws⟩ *awās* "now" ŠKZ 29, ŠH 11, BM 11, NPi 5 a11,05, 33 f13,03 (MPa ⟨ʾwʾs⟩); ⟨ʾwstm⟩ *ustam* "last"[30] NPi 8 b2,02 (MPa ⟨ʿstym⟩); ⟨ʾwnt⟩ *awand* "so much, so great" ŠKZ 3, 16, 17, 29 (MPa ⟨ʾwynd⟩); ⟨ʾwtyn⟩ *āwadīn* "such, so long" ŠKZ 22 (MPa ⟨ʾwdyn, ʾʾwdyn⟩); ⟨byš⟩ *wēč/bēč* "more, much"[31] ŠKZ 16, ŠH 7 (MPa ⟨byc, byz:⟩); ⟨hndymn⟩ *handēmān* "in the presence of" NPi 15 c10,03

---

[29] Gignoux 1972a, p. 45, translated it as "volontiers". See fn. 69 for the meaning of *āgām* as "or".

[30] It occurs in the syntagm ⟨HN ʾwstm⟩ *yad ustam* "till the last" < OIr. **ustama-*. See Skjærvø 1983c, p. 52, and fn. 71 in this work.

[31] MPa ⟨wyš⟩ occurs in Durkin-Meisterernst 2004, p. 358, as follows: "Pa wyš Correct? M1214 2a".

(MPa ⟨hndymʾn, hndymʾʾn⟩); ⟨hyp⟩ *hēb* ŠKZ 19, ŠH 12, 13, ŠTBq 6, NPi 17 c2,05, 25 e3,01 (particle of exhortation[32], MPa ⟨hyb⟩); ⟨kd⟩ *kad* "when" ŠKZ 17 (MPa ⟨kd⟩); ⟨nhwšt⟩ *naxwišt* "first(ly)" ŠKZ 3, NPi 26 e12,02, 27 e4,03, 38 g7,02 (MPa ⟨nxwšt⟩); ⟨prhš⟩ *frāč* "forward, forth" ŠKZ 2, NPi 17 c1,05, 22 d13,04, 25 e5,01 (MPa ⟨frʾc⟩);[33] ⟨prybr⟩ *par^{i}wār* "around"[34] ŠKZ 5 (6x), 6 (10x), 7 (11x), 8 (10x), 9, 12 (7x), 13 (10x), 14 (8x), 15 (8x); ⟨šwgwn⟩ *čawāgōn* "as, like, of such a kind, how" ŠKZ 29, NPi 17 c5,05 [⟨[šw]gwn⟩], 18 c1,06, 24 d14,06, 32 f2,05 (MPa ⟨cwʾgwn⟩).

There are two alleged exceptions. Firstly, the adverb-adjective ⟨hmy⟩, which is attested once in AW 4 and certainly has the final -y# (see Plate IV). In Gignoux 1972a, p. 52, IPa ⟨hmy⟩ is compared with IMP ⟨hmy⟩ *ham* "also" (and ⟨hmy gwnky⟩ *ham gōnag* "in the same way")[35], cf. MPa ⟨hm⟩ *ham*. Nevertheless, the Parthian form in AW 4 can also be read as *hamē*, as Nyberg 1923, p. 204, did, with the old meaning "same, too". In this way, it would be compared with the same word occuring in MPa ⟨hmyw, hmyyw⟩ *hamēw* (modern meaning "always"), and then the final -y# would indicate the long vowel *-ē* in a final position. Thus, ⟨hmy⟩ could be read as *hamē* in Inscriptional Parthian (< OIr. **hama-* + *a̯iu̯a-* "one"[36] or rather + **a̯iu-* "time"[37]). However, it is not easy to understand why the Inscriptional Parthian form would have avoided the "historical writting" with a final ⟨-w⟩, which was still pronounced in Manichaean Parthian (⟨hmyw, hmyyw⟩) [!]. IPa ⟨hmy⟩ (only in AW 4) may be considered an exception of an adverb taking the final -y#. In any case, the interpretation of the passage remains not conclusive (cf. Skjærvø 1995, p. 290).

A further possible exception is the preposition ⟨pty⟩ *pad* (MPa ⟨pd, pṭ⟩) "in, on, by" (ŠH 6, 11, BM 6, 11, 21, ŠKZ 3, 4, 5 and *passim*, NPi 2 a11,02, 4 a6,04, 7 b2,01 and *passim*, Nisā 658/5, 1379/7), which always ends in -y#.[38] This preposition comes from OIr. **pati* (cf. OP *patiy*, Av. *paiti*). The

32 About this particle, see Skjærvø 1983c, p. 39.

33 As Skjærvø 1983c, p. 71, has shown, the comparative form that Gignoux 1972a, p. 60, read in NPi as †⟨prhštr-n⟩ *frāžtar-* + the enclitic prounoun *ān/an*, is an incorrect transliteration of ⟨prhš⟩ (NPi 17 c1,05) + ⟨(hyp)⟩ (NPi 17 c2,05).

34 Cf. IMP ⟨prwʾry⟩ *parwār* < OIr. **pari-bāra-* (Back 1978, p. 246).

35 Cf. Huyse 2003, p. 66, fn. 87.

36 Huyse 2003, p. 70.

37 Bartholomae 1920, p. 26 f.

38 This preposition is always Aramaeographically spelt in Inscriptional Middle Persian: ⟨PWN⟩ *pad*.

presence of the final -y# in this preposition can be explained as a historical spelling of an OIr. **-i*. As professor Cantera has suggested to me, its proclitical position in the phonic chain could have contributed to a longer preservation of the final *-i*.[39]

2.2.2. VERBAL INFLECTIONAL FORMS AND INFINITIVES

Inscriptional Parthian -y# does not occur in either the verbal inflectional forms or in the active infinitives.

The following list shows the inflected verbal forms:[40]

- ***Ind. 3sg.***[41] ⟨ʾst⟩ *ast* "there is" Nisā 2120/8 (MPa ⟨ʾ(ʾ)st⟩), ⟨hnbndYWd⟩ *hanbandēd*[(?)] "he organizes" NPi 16 c7,04,[42] ⟨kʾmYWt⟩ *kāmēd* "he wishes"[43] NPi 30 e13,06, 32 f7,02 (MPa ⟨kʾmyd⟩), ⟨krhyd⟩ *karīhēd* "it is done" ŠKZ 19 (cf. IMP ⟨klyty⟩), ⟨nytprYWt⟩ *nidfārēd* "he hastes" NPi 21 d1,03 (MPa ⟨nydfʾryd⟩), ⟨prtšYWt⟩ *pardačēd* "he remains" ŠKZ 22, ⟨ptyʾwyd⟩[44] *pattāwēd* "he endures" ŠKZ 22 (cf. IMP ⟨ptwdʾt⟩), ⟨pywdYWt⟩[45] **parrūdēd*[(??)] "he besieges" ŠKZ 9,

---

39 This possibility has to be related to certain Parthian compounds with the first member ending in ⟨y⟩, which I hope to deal with in a forthcoming paper.

40 The semi-Aramaeographic transliterations of verbs with a ⟨YW⟩ element follow the principles established by Durkin-Meisterernst 2000, p. 75-81. Former scholars did not use this convention.

41 The form NPi 32 f2,02 ⟨šʾYWt⟩ is considered by Gignoux 1972a, p. 64, a 3sg. "qu'il puisse" (transliterated ⟨šʾywt⟩). However, the context points to a past participle ⟨ʾk [...] OBDt W šʾYWt HWYndy⟩ *ag [...] kird ud šāhād*[??] *ahēndē* "if [...] he had done and [had] been able", thus Skjærvø 1983c, p. 108; 1989, p. 336. The instance of NPi 37 g2,01 ⟨prksYWt⟩ is probaby also a past participle *pargast* (cf. MPa ⟨prgst⟩), see Skjærvø 1983b, p. 119. For its origin in OIr. **pari-kas-*, see Gignoux 1972a, p. 60 (fn. 88) and Skjærvø 1983c, p. 115.

42 See Skjærvø 1983b, p. 43; 1983c, p. 69-70. Different from Gignoux 1972a, p. 49, and Henning 1958, p. 34: †⟨HN ONOYWd⟩.

43 NPi 30 e13,06, 32 f7,02 ⟨kʾmywt⟩ is considered an ind. 3sg. by Skjærvø 1983b, p. 133, and Gignoux 1972a, p. 55. For its interpretation as a past participle, see Ferrer-Losilla 2013, p. 191.

44 The second ⟨y⟩ in ⟨ptyʾwyd⟩ could be an Aramaeographic element: ⟨ptyʾwYd⟩. Huyse 1999, Band 1, p. 52, transcribes *pattāwēd*. As Skjærvø 1983c, p. 114 (fn. 43) pointed out, ⟨ptyʾwyd⟩ could be considered a mistake instead of [+]⟨ptyʾwywd⟩ (ind./subj. 3sg., cf. IMP ⟨ptwdʾt⟩ *pattāyād*).

45 Huyse 1999, Band 1, p. 73 and Band 2, p. 33, emends in [+]⟨prwdywt⟩ (even [+]⟨prywdywt⟩) and transcribes **parrūδīd*. The form is suspected to be a past

⟨twhšYWd⟩ *tuxšēd* "he strives" ŠKZ 30 (MPa ⟨twxšyd⟩), ⟨zʾmYWd⟩[46] *žāmēd* "he sends" ŠH 14, ŠTBq 6 (MPa ⟨jʾmyd⟩, < OIr. **ǰāmai̯a-* "to cause to go");

- ***Ind. 3pl.*** ⟨ptʾpYWnt⟩ **pattābēnd* "they brand"[47] NPi 20 d14,02 (cf. MPa ind. 3sg. ⟨ptʾbyd⟩), ⟨wysdYWnt⟩ *wisēdānd/wisēdēnd* "they will depart"[48] NPi 21 d11,03 (cf. MPa ⟨wsyd, wsyyd⟩), ⟨rʾYWn(t)⟩ **rāyēnd* "they arrange" NPi 9 b9,03[49];
- ***Ind. 1pl.*** ⟨twhšYWm⟩ *tuxšām* "we strive" ŠKZ 29 (MPa ⟨twxšʾm⟩), ⟨ʾwpdysYWm⟩ *abdēsām* "we order" ŠKZ 19 (present stem MPa ⟨ʾbdys-⟩).

Although scarcely attested, Inscriptional Parthian phonographic infinitives do not have -y# either. The infinitive ending OIr. **-tanai̯* (an old dative ending) would still have yielded *-tan/-dan* in Proto-Parthian, so a final -y# would be unexpected in the infinitives. Thus, the infinitive ending in ⟨-tn⟩ *-tan/-dan* appears always without -y#: ⟨prmYtn⟩ *framādan*[50] "to order" NPi 4 a11-12,04 [⟨prmY(tn)⟩], 31 f7,01, 34 f3,04, 38 g15,02 (MPa ⟨frmʾdn⟩), ⟨wyzʾwytn⟩[51] *wizāwīdan* "to do harm" NPi 9 b7,03 (MPa present stem ⟨wyzʾw-⟩ "to extinguish"), ⟨rhtn⟩ *raxtan*[52] "to fight, hasten" NPi 21 d1,03. It should be noted that the form †⟨kwštny⟩ *kuštan* "to fight, to kill" listed by Gignoux 1972a, p. 55, is to be read as a past participle:

---

participle, see Skjærvø 1989, p. 336.

46 BM 14 ⟨zymYWt⟩.

47 In Gignoux 1972a, p. 61, it is considered a 3pl.: " 'ils marquent' (au fer rouge)". However, since the word is followed by ⟨MSGYWt⟩ (a finite verb or a past participle), Skjærvø 1983b, p. 79, thinks of a noun "branding" or of an adjective *pattāb-wand* "branded".

48 Probably subj. 3pl., see Skjærvø 1983c, p. 67, 80, 107. *Corrig.* Gignoux 1972a, p. 68, †⟨YSDYWnt⟩.

49 Its meaning is uncertain, cf. Skjærvø 1983c, p. 57. Absent in Gignoux 1972a.

50 Since ⟨prmytn⟩ is not the usual spelling for *framādan* (cf. MPa ⟨frmʾdn⟩), Skjærvø 1983c, p. 35, thinks it may represent **framāyādan* (or even **framīdan*) with a secondary past stem. As prof. Desmond Durkin-Meisterernst suggested to me in Cracow (September 9th, 2011, ECIS 7), the unexpected ⟨y⟩ of ⟨prmYtn⟩ could be an Aramaeographic element, as well as the ⟨YW⟩ element in some of the present stems listed in 1.2 (cf. Durkin-Meisterernst 2000).

51 Gignoux 1972a, p. 67, †⟨wyzʾdytn⟩ "nuire" must be read as ⟨wyzʾwytn⟩ (NPi 9 b7, 03) with the same meaning as Inscriptional Middle Persian ⟨wzʾdtny⟩ "to destroy" (NPi 10 B11,05, 12 C6-7,01), see Skjærvø 1983b, p. 36.

52 About its possible etymon, see Skjærvø 1983c, p. 79.

NPi 27 e4,03 ⟨nhwšt kwšt [W?] MNW r⟩ (*apud* Skjærvø 1983b, p. 56).

As expected, the Aramaeographic infinitives have a phonographic complement without -y#, see the forms in 1.2.

3. PHONOGRAPHIC FORMS: THE NOMINAL INFLECTION

The analysis of the distribution of -y# must be limited to the scope of the phonographic forms of the nominal inflection. As Back 1978 and Huyse 2003 did for the Inscriptional Middle Persian vocabulary, I have also classified the Inscriptional Parthian nominal forms, according to the number of their syllables, into monosyllables and polysyllables. Since -y# is not assumed to have had any phonetic value, as pointed out in 0.2, it is not counted as an independent syllable.

3.1. PRESENCE OR ABSENCE OF FINAL –*y* IN MONOSYLLABIC NOUNS

The lists of the monosyllabic words classified according to the absence or presence of -y# are presented below. A summary overview shows that the main bulk of Inscriptional Parthian monosyllabic nouns do not have -y#, as opposed to Inscriptional Middle Persian, in which the monosyllabic words generally do have it (Huyse 2003, p. 29).

The following list shows the Inscriptional Parthian monosyllables which do not accept the -y#: ⟨bʾz⟩ *bāz*[53] "tribute" ŠKZ 3, 4; ⟨gryw⟩ *grīw* (a grain measure) ŠKZ 20, 22, 29 (=MPa); ⟨gtw⟩ [historical spelling] *gāh* "throne" NPi 23 d3,05, 31 f1,02 [⟨(g)t(w)⟩], 40 g4,04 (MPa ⟨gʾẖ⟩, cf. IMP ⟨gʾsy⟩); ⟨gwt⟩ *gōt/gōd* "Goths" ŠKZ 3; ⟨gyʾn⟩ *gyān* "soul" ŠKZ 4, DE 55,1, 55,2 (=MPa); ⟨hw⟩ *hō* "he, this" ŠKZ 11, 19, ŠH 12, 13, BM 12, 13, ŠTBq 6 (=MPa); ⟨pʾrs⟩ *pārs* "Persia" ŠKZ 1, 11, 16, NPi 6 a11,06, 15 c4,03 (pl. ⟨pʾrsʾn, pʾrsn⟩; =MPa); ⟨pʾs⟩ *pās* (a liquid measure) ŠKZ 20, 22, 29; ⟨pwšt⟩ *pušt* "protection, support" ŠKZ 17, NPi 18 c10,06, 32 f12,02, 40 g10,04 (=MPa); ⟨rʾm⟩ *rām* "peace(ful)" NPi 31 f6,01 (=MPa); ⟨rʾšt⟩ *rāšt* "right, true" NPi 32 f2,02, 36 f3,06 (=MPa); ⟨šʾt⟩ *šād* "happy" NPi 40 g9,04 (MPa ⟨šʾd⟩); ⟨twhm⟩ *tōhm* "seed, family" NPi 3 a12,03, 28 e12,04, 36 f8,06 (MPa ⟨twhm, twxm⟩); ⟨wym⟩ *wēm* "rock, stone" ŠH 6, 12, BM 6, 12, 21 (=MPa); ⟨yʾt⟩ *yād* "portion" AW 2 (MPa ⟨yʾd⟩); ⟨bg⟩ *bag* "god, divine" ŠH 4, BM 4, 18 (MPa ⟨bg, bγ⟩); ⟨rnz⟩ *ranǰ* "toil, labour" NPi 32 f7,02 (MPa ⟨rnj⟩); ⟨hrw⟩ *harw* "every, all" ŠKZ 3, 11, 19 (=MPa); ⟨mrz⟩ *marz* "border, boundary" ŠKZ 2, 3 (=MPa); ⟨hštr⟩ *(h)šahr* "land, country" ŠKZ 2, 3 and

[53] Probably related to MPa ⟨bxš-⟩ *baxš-* "to divide, distribute".

passim, NPi 8 b2,02, 28 e4,04 and *passim* (MPa ⟨šhr⟩); ⟨np⟩ *năβ*(?) [or *nāf* ?] "family" Nisā N. 307/2 (cf. MPa ⟨nʾf⟩ *nāf*); ⟨pnd⟩ "counsel" NPi 9 b8,03, 9 b10,03 (=MPa); ⟨prtw⟩ *pahr(w)* [for this reading, see 4.4.2.1] "Parthians, Parthia" NPi 4 a5,04, 6 a11,06, 15 c4,03, 34 f6,04, ŠKZ 1, 16 (IPa pl. ⟨(p)rt(wʾ)[n]⟩ [NPi 2 a17,02]; cf. MPa ⟨phrwg⟩); ⟨šhr⟩ ŠTBq 2, ŠVŠ 5, 7, 12 and ⟨šyhr⟩ ANRm 2, ŠKZ 1, ŠNRb 3, ŠH 2, 4, BM 2, 4, 16, 18 *čihr* "nature, seed" (MPa ⟨cyhr⟩); ⟨wrt⟩ *ward*[54] "stone" ŠTBq 4, 5; ⟨yʾzt⟩ *yazd* "god" ŠKZ 17, 30 (MPa ⟨yzd⟩[55], cf. IPa ob.pl. ⟨yʾztn⟩); ⟨znb⟩ *zanb* "edge, bank" ŠKZ 19 (cf. IMP ⟨dnby⟩, Sgd. ⟨zmb⟩)[56]; ⟨znk⟩ *zang* "kind, sort" ŠH 8, BM 8, NPi 29 e13,05 (=MPa).

The list of monosyllables which do accept -y# is more reduced:[57] ⟨ʾry⟩ *ar/er* "noble, iranian" ŠKZ 19 (ob.pl. ⟨ʾryʾn⟩ *aryān*); ⟨hwry⟩ *xwar/xur* (an alcoholic drink) Nisā 950/1, 1730/4 (cf. MMP ⟨xwr⟩ *xur*); ⟨wty⟩[58] *wad* "bad" NPi 15 c15,03, 18 c2,06 (MPa ⟨wd⟩); ⟨kʾry⟩ *kār* "work, task" NPi 4 a11,04, 38 g15,02 (MPa ⟨kʾr, kʾʾr, qʾr⟩); ⟨kpy⟩ *kab*[59] ŠKZ 2; ⟨mry⟩ *mar* (measure of liquids) Nisā *passim* (cf. MMP ⟨mr⟩ "number, account, class"); ⟨rpy⟩ *rab/raβ* "attack" ŠKZ 11 (MPa ⟨rf, rβ⟩); ⟨šyty⟩ *čid*[60] "gathering, collection (of

---

54 From OIr. **u̯arta-* (cf. Av. *varəta-* which yields Kurdish *bard*), see MacKenzie 1999, p. 81.

55 Durkin-Meisterernst 2004, p. 376, transcribes *yazad*, both for Manichaean Middle Persian and Manichaean Parthian.

56 Possibly related to Av. *zamb-*, OInd. *jambh-* "to show the teeth". See Back 1978, p. 207.

57 The word ⟨(s)wty⟩ (Gignoux 1972a, p. 64) *sūd* "profit, benefit" is difficult to evaluate in such a damaged passage, NPi 38 g6,02. Skjærvø 1983c, p. 116, comments: "This stone has been seen by Rawlinson only; ⟨pwty⟩ may have been misread for ⟨pty⟩ (…)".

58 *Corrig.* Gignoux 1972a, p. 54, †⟨(h)wty⟩.

59 With ⟨ΘORA⟩ *kōf* "mountain": *kab kōf* = "Caucasus" (Gr. ΚΑΠ·ΟΡΟΥΣ).

60 The root of IPa ⟨šyty⟩ and IMP ⟨cytʾky, cyty⟩ is the same (MacKenzie 1999, p. 76): **čai̯-* "to heap up, gather, collect" (Cheung 2007, p. 26). On the one hand, the transcription of IMP ⟨cytʾky⟩ as *čēdāg* is assumed by MacKenzie (*ibid.*) because of the Baločī forms *čēdag*, *čēδāg*, which were taken to be Persian loanwords in Baločī. On the other hand, Back 1978, p. 206, seems to prefer a transcription *čīdāg* < **čītākā-*. However, there is no reason to read the MP infinitive ⟨cytn'⟩ and the past participle IPa ⟨šyty⟩/ IMP ⟨cyty⟩ with a long root vowel. Mackenzie 1971, p. 22, and Nyberg 1974, p. 55-56, transcribed *čīdan*, and it seems that this transcription with a long root vowel is due to a (mistaken) comparison with the many verbs whose infinitive ends in *-īdan*. OIr. root **čai̯-* would have created an infinitive **čitanai̯*, which would have

stones)" ŠH 7, 9, 10, 13, ŠTBq 5, 6, BM 7, 9, 10, 13 (cf. IMP ⟨cytʾky⟩).

3.1.1. Distribution of final *–y* in monosyllabic nouns

It seems there is a distribution of -y# in monosyllabic words that depends on the syllabic weight.

Monosyllabic words containing a long vowel *natura*, which is generally indicated by the *matres lectionis*, do not have the final -y#: ⟨bʾz⟩ *bāz*, ⟨gryw⟩ *grīw*, ⟨gyʾn⟩ *gyān*, ⟨pʾrs⟩ *pārs*, ⟨rʾm⟩ *rām*, ⟨rʾšt⟩ *rāšt*, ⟨šʾt⟩ *šād*, ⟨wym⟩ *wēm*, etc. Furthermore, the monosyllabic words containing a long syllable *positione*, that is, a short vowel followed by two or more consonants, do not have -y# either: ⟨rnz⟩ *ranǰ*, ⟨mrz⟩ *marz*, ⟨hštr⟩ *(h)šahr*, ⟨šyhr⟩ *čihr*, ⟨wrt⟩ *ward*, ⟨znb⟩ *zanb*, ⟨znk⟩ *zang*, etc. (see above 3.1).

Furthermore, Inscriptional Parthian monosyllabic words containing a short vowel not followed by two (or more) consonants always have -y#: ⟨hwry⟩ *xwar/xur*, ⟨mry⟩ *mar*, ⟨rpy⟩ *rab/raβ*, ⟨wty⟩ *wad* ... (see above 3.1).

Hence a first rule can be stated: Inscriptional Parthian monosyllables containing a long vowel *natura* or *positione* do not have -y#, whereas the final -y# appears in monosyllables with a short vowel not followed by two or more consonants.

3.1.2. Exceptions

There are only a few exceptions to this rule: ⟨bg⟩ *bag*, ⟨np⟩ *nă̄β*[(?)] and ⟨kʾry⟩ *kār*.

---

yielded ZMP **čidan* ⟨cytn'⟩, and a past participle **čita-*, which would have yielded MP and IPa **čid*. The non-etymological lengthening of *i* and *u* in many Middle (and Modern) Persian words has been recently studied by Korn 2009. According to this scholar (Korn 2009, p. 205ff.), the lengthening of *i* and *u* occurred in the final position of a word preceding voiced stops, and only in polysyllabic words. A possible counterexample (Korn 2009, p. 203) is Middle Persian *čīd* vs. Old Indian *citá-*. I am not sure whether this lengthening also took place in Parthian: the *scriptio plena* in IPa ⟨šyty⟩ may reflect a long or a short vowel. Nonetheless, the verbal form from the present stem of MPa *čīn-*/ *čin-*, ⟨cnynd⟩ (1x) could be an argument for transcribing a short vowel *činēnd* (although ⟨cynynd⟩ is also attested once), since in Manichaean Parthian the *scriptio plena* would be expected for a long vowel (the form MPa ⟨cynynd⟩ can be read with both a short or long vowel). Furthermore (*apud* Korn 2009, p. 209), the Baločī –a North-Western Iranian language– also has a short vowel in this root: *čit* (and *gičit*) and a present stem *čin-* (and *gičin-*).

The presence of -y# in ⟨kʾry⟩, where a long vowel is guaranteed (cf. MPa ⟨kʾʾr, kʾr, qʾr⟩), can be explained as a historical spelling if it is derived from OIr. **kārii̯a-* (Henning 1958, p. 64). Nevertheless, such a form does not occur in either Old Persian or in Avestan.[61]

For the word ⟨bg⟩ *bag* (<**baga-*) "god, divine" (MPa ⟨bg, bγ⟩) I have just one *ad hoc* explanation. This word is attested only once in the inscription of Šābuhr at Hājjīābād (line 4), whereas all the other versions of this inscription have the Aramaeogram ⟨ALHA⟩. In the same inscription, *bag* is attested as an epithet of the proper name of the king: ŠH 1 and ŠTBq 1 ⟨ALHA šhypwhr⟩ *bag šă^{h}buhr*, ŠH 4 and ŠTBq 2 ⟨ALHA ʾrthštr⟩ *bag ardaxšahr*, ŠH 4 ⟨bg pʾpk⟩ and ŠTBq 3 ⟨ALHA pʾpk⟩ *bag pābag*. In such instances, *bag* seems to function as the first element of a compound to which the name of the king is added (cf. *kayxosrō* < **kau̯$^{(i)}$-husrāu̯-*).[62] The groups *bag-šă^{h}buhr*, *bag-pābag*, *bag-ardaxšahr* would be single words, that is, compounds. Since *bag* was not an independent noun, it did not have -y# (cf. the proper name NPi 25 e13,01 ⟨bgš[hypwhr]⟩[63] *bagšă^{h}buhr*).[64] Rather than being a compound, Desmond Durkin-Meisterernst has suggested to me that ⟨bg⟩ could be the development of an ancient vocative.[65] The explanations are both plausible.

The form ⟨np⟩ *năb/ năβ* will be explained in paragraph 4.2.

3.2. PRESENCE OR ABSENCE OF FINAL –*y* IN POLYSYLLABIC NOUNS

Since the distribution of the -y# seems to be related to the weight of the syllable, at least in the monosyllabic nouns, I have classified the polysyllabic nouns into groups according to two principles: the presence or absence

---

61 One could also assume a femenine **kārii̯ā-*.

62 In his presentation in Cracow called "The Paikuli Monument and its Inscription" (September 7th, 2011, ECIS 7), Professor Carlo Cereti also considered that the name *bag-šābuhr* is a dvandva compound. See also Zimmer 1984.

63 The reconstruction of the Inscriptional Parthian version is quite probable, if it translates the Middle Persian title of NPi 27 E11,04 ⟨bgšhpwhr[y]⟩ (also in NPi 27 E16,04 ⟨bgš(hp)[whry]⟩).

64 In my opinion, the spelling ⟨g⟩ in Inscriptional Parthian and in Inscriptional Middle Persian cannot represent the pronunciation of Middle Persian *bay*, cf. MPa ⟨bg, bγ⟩.

65 Cf. Sogdian, where ⟨bg⟩ appears as an enclitic (loosing its vocative ending).

of -y# and the weight of the final syllable of the word[66] (long final syllable *natura* or *positione*, and short final syllable with a short vowel not followed by two or more consonants).

3.2.1. CLASSIFICATION OF POLYSYLLABLES WITHOUT *–y*

Since the group of words that do not contain the -y# is far more numerous than those words containing it, I begin with the classification of the words without -y# according to the weight of the final syllable. Firstly, I offer the list of the words with a final long syllable *natura* (3.2.1.1); secondly, the list of the words with a final long syllable *positione* (3.2.1.2); and finally, the list of the words with a final short syllable –short vowel followed by just one consonant– (3.2.1.3).

3.2.1.1. Polysyllables with a long final syllable natura

The group of polysyllables with a long final syllable *natura* is the most numerous. They do not usually contain -y#:

a. Common nouns

Common nouns appear: ⟨ʾbdyn⟩ *abdēn* "custom, habit; usual" ŠKZ 19 (MPa ⟨ʾbdyn, ʾbdyyn⟩); ⟨ʾbgm⟩ *abgām* "pain, agony" NPi 32 f8,02 (MPa ⟨ʾbgʾm⟩[67]); ⟨ʾbykškn⟩ **abkašgān* "next to the plowed fields"[68] AW 2, 7; [⟨ʾkm⟩ *āgām* †"willing";][69] ⟨ʾpʾryk⟩ *abārīg* "other" NPi 9 b5-6,03, 15 c3,03 (MPa ⟨ʾbʾryg⟩); ⟨ʾrwʾn⟩ *arwān* "soul" ŠKZ 18, 19, 22 (MPa ⟨ʾrwʾn⟩ and ⟨rwʾn⟩ *ruwān*); ⟨ʾwʾr⟩ **awwār* "robbery, predatory/ booty" ŠKZ 16, NPi 21 d1,03 (cf. MPa ⟨ʾywʾr⟩ *ēwār* [and ⟨ʾpr⟩ *appar*]?);[70] ⟨ʾwpsyk⟩ **ōbsīg*? "tax" (?) Nisā 813/1; [⟨ʾwstm⟩ **awistām* (??) "column, pillar" (cf.

---

66 In words with a final -y#, the final syllable is the one preceding the -y#.

67 Durkin-Meisterernst 2004, p. 10 (with bibliography), attaches a question mark to the transcription of this word: "ʾ**bgʾm 1** Pa /abγām/? '*grant, *a thing given'."

68 It may be a plural form. Henning 1958, p. 31 (fn. 1), derives it from **abi* + *kr̥ša* (Av. *karša-*) + the adjective ending *-akān*.

69 This interpretation was connected with MPa ⟨ʾgʾmʾy, ʾqʾmʾy⟩ *agāmāy* "unwilling(ly)" (Gignoux 1972a, p. 45), but it is clear that the meaning of IPa ⟨ʾkm⟩ *āgām* (MPa ⟨ʾgʾm⟩) is "or", as Skjærvø 1983c, p. 111 (with bibliography) has pointed out. See fn. 29.

70 From OIr. **apa-bāra-*? For the meaning "booty" < OIr. **adi-u̯āra-*, see MacKenzie 1982, p. 283. MPa ⟨ʾpr⟩ *appar* "predatory, thievish" could be derived from another form. Back 1978, p. 176-177, discussed IMP ⟨*ʾpʾry/*ʾdwʾry/ʾdʾly⟩, IPa ⟨ʾwʾr⟩, hardly criticized by MacKenzie (*ibid.*).

MMP ⟨ʾwy(s)[tʾm]⟩ *awestām*);][71] ⟨ʾwstykn⟩ *ōstīgān* "firm, sure" NPi 3 a16,03 (MPa ⟨ʾwstygʾn⟩); ⟨ʾwyrn⟩ *awērān* "ruin, destruction" ŠKZ 5, 12 (cf. IMP ⟨ʾwylʾn, ʾwdylʾn⟩)[72]; ⟨ʾwzmn⟩ **užmān* "*trial"[73] NPi 8 b12,02 (cf. IMP ⟨ʾwzmʾn⟩); ⟨ʾzʾt⟩ *āzād* "noble, free" NPi 3 a13,03 [⟨ʾz(ʾ)t⟩], 15 c1,03, 34 f8,04, 38 g2,02 (MPa ⟨ʾzʾd⟩); ⟨bwdystn⟩ *bōdestān* "verger, garden" Nisā 767/3 (MPa ⟨bwdystʾn⟩); ⟨byʾspn⟩ *bayaspān* "menssenger (of the king), envoy" NPi 22 d9,04 (cf. MMP ⟨byʾspʾn⟩); ⟨dnk⟩ *dānāg* "wise (man)" DE 56 (cf. MMP ⟨dʾnʾg⟩); ⟨dpyr⟩ *dibīr* "scribe" DE 56 (MPa ⟨dbyr⟩); ⟨dstnypyk⟩ *dastnibēg* "handwritten" ŠKZ 30 (MPa ⟨nbyg⟩ *nibēg* "writing, book, document"); ⟨dynr⟩ *dēnār* "dinar" ŠKZ 4 (MPa ⟨dynʾr⟩); ⟨grbn⟩ *grīwān* (a grain measure; cf. IPa and MPa ⟨gryw⟩ *grīw*) DE 1,1, 2,11; ⟨hykmwn⟩ *hēgemōn* "leader, head" (Gr. ἩΓΕΜΩΝ) ŠKZ 11; ⟨hmyʾbdyn⟩ *hamabdēn* "with same custom, habit" NPi 15 c7,03; ⟨hmysʾk⟩ *hamesāg* "total" ŠKZ 9, 15 (MPa ⟨sʾg⟩ *sāg* "number, part"); ⟨hngwšn⟩ *hangōšn* (or *hangōšān* ?) "crossroads" ŠKZ 3 (cf. MMP ⟨gwšg⟩ *gōšag* "corner"); ⟨hnsk⟩ **hansāg* "building" (?)[74] AS 4; ⟨hrtyk⟩ *hridīg* "third" ŠKZ 9 (MPa ⟨hrdyg⟩); ⟨hštrʾhmr⟩ *(h)šahrāhmār* "(room) of the county accounts" NPi 14 c14,02 (cf. IPa ⟨ʾhmrkr⟩ "accountant"); ⟨hštrstn⟩ *(h)šahrestān* "region, province, city" NPi 26 e3,02 (MPa ⟨šhrystʾn⟩); ⟨hwpn⟩ *hōfān*[75] (measure) ŠKZ 20, 22, 29; ⟨kʾrwʾn⟩ *kārwān* "army (on the march)" NPi 13 c4,01, 21 d9,03 (MPa ⟨kʾrwʾn, qʾrwʾn⟩); ⟨kwpdʾr⟩ *kōfdār* "mountain-dweller" NPi 8 b10,02 (cf. IMP ⟨kwpdʾly⟩); ⟨mdkdr⟩[76] **madugdār* "cupbearer" ŠKZ 24

---

[71] This interpretation was made by Gignoux 1972a, p. 48. The passage of NPi 8 b2,02, where IPa ⟨ʾwstm⟩ occurs, is as damaged as the form in the MMP text: ⟨[d](st) ʾwy(s)[tʾm]⟩ "hand support" (see Durkin-Meisterernst 2004, p. 76). Skjærvø 1983c, p. 52, has no doubt that the passage of NPi ⟨HN ʾwstm⟩ *yad ustam* means "till the last" < **ustama-* (cf. MPa ⟨ʿstym⟩ *istem* "lastly"). See fn. 30.

[72] It comes from OIr. **abi-u̯ari̯āna-* (*apud* Back 1978, p. 194).

[73] Gignoux 1972a, p. 48, interprets it as *ō-žamān* "in that time" but, as Skjærvø 1983c, p. 55, pointed out, the Parthian expression would be *hō-žamān*. I share Skjærvø's assumption of a parallel form to *framān* (from *framūdan*), so here we have **uzmān* (from *uzmūdān/azmūdān* "to try").

[74] Gignoux 1972a, p. 52, translated it as "edifice, construction (?)". Henning 1952a, p. 176, as "erection", linking this word to Sogdian ⟨ʾnsʾʾk⟩ (<**ham-sāka-*) "prepared things, provisions".

[75] Gignoux 1972a, p. 53, transcribes *hōfan*, but Huyse 1999, Band 2, p. 114, *hōfān*.

[76] Gignoux 1972a, p. 57, transliterates †⟨mdwdr⟩, but as Huyse 1999, Band 1, p. 56, pointed out, there is a ⟨k⟩ to be read with certainty in this form,

(cf. IMP ⟨mdʾly⟩ *mayār*); ⟨mdwstn⟩ *madustān* (*/madestān*) "wine store" Nisā 90/5, 1609/2,4, 1693/2,4; ⟨mhymʾn⟩ **mehmān* "of a great House"[77] NPi 41 g7,05 (cf. IMP ⟨myhmʾn⟩); ⟨mrzwpn⟩ *marzōbān/marzbān*[78] "protector of the border, margrave" Nisā 1899/3 (cf. MMP ⟨mrzbʾn⟩ *marzbān*); ⟨mzdyzn⟩[79] *mazdēzn* "mazdean" ANRm1, ŠH 1, 3, NPi 1 a5,01 [⟨mz(dyz)n⟩], ŠKZ 1, 19, ŠNRb 1, 2, ŠVŠ 4, 6 (cf. IMP ⟨mzdysn⟩); ⟨mzn⟩ *mazān* "principal" Nisā 525/2, 672/2, 675/3, 916/2; ⟨nhwdr⟩ *naxwadār* "prefect"[80] KJ̌l 2 (cf. IPa ⟨nhwšt⟩ and MPa ⟨nxwšt⟩ *naxwišt* "first(ly)"); ⟨nnystnkn⟩ **nanēstangān*? "Nanaia's temple" Nisā 228/2, 1682/3; ⟨nymstyk⟩ *nimastīg* "supplication" ŠKZ 4 (MPa ⟨nmstyg⟩); ⟨pʾšnʾm⟩ **pādnām* "reputation" ŠKZ 18, 19 (cf. IMP ⟨ptnʾm⟩);[81] ⟨pdys⟩ *pă̄dēs*[82] "counsel, instruction, command" NPi 4 a16,04, 9 b8,03, 43 g4/07 (MPa ⟨ʾbdys⟩ *abdēs*); ⟨prmtr⟩ *framādār* "commander, ruler" ŠKZ 26, 28 (cf. ZMP ⟨plmʾtʾl⟩); ⟨prnwš⟩ **parnō̆š* "old" AR 8; ⟨pryʾt⟩ *frayād* "aid, help" NPi 16 c14,04, 19 d3,01 (cf. MPa ⟨fryʾd-⟩ "to come to the aid of"); ⟨ptgm⟩ *padgām* "message" NPi 16 c15,04, 27 e13,03, 34 f6,04, 35 f3,05, 38 g4,02 (MPa ⟨pdgʾm⟩); ⟨ptsyk, ptysyk⟩ *padsēg* "compensation, equivalent"[83] Nisā 22/2, 32/1 and *passim*; ⟨(p)tydymn⟩[84] *paddēmān* "face to face" ŠKZ 3;

---

cf. ⟨mdkdr⟩ (see Fig. VI). The form ⟨mdʾly⟩ *may(y)ār* comes from **maδ-δār-* <**madu-dāra-* in Inscriptional Middle Persian (Back 1978, p. 229), while the Parthian form would come from **maduka-dāra-*.

77 Thus Skjærvø 1983c, p. 124.

78 For the transcription *marzōbān* (<**marza-* + *-au̯a-* + *pāna-* ?) cf. the Arabian loanword *marzubān* reported by Nyberg 1974, p. 127.

79 IPa 10x ⟨mzdyzn⟩, but 2x ⟨mzdzny⟩ (ŠTBq 1, 2). The two forms with final -y# are transliterated by Gignoux 1972a, p. 59, and MacKenzie 1999, p. 81, but not by Back 1978, p. 372, who transliterates ⟨mzdyzn⟩. MacKenzie (*ibid.*) indicates that "Gropp's [GROPP, G. *Einige neuentdeckte Inschriften aus sasanidischer Zeit*, in HINZ, W. (1969) *Altiranische Funde und Forschungen*, Berlin. Ch. X, 229-237] reading *mzdzny* is correct". I could not find a photograph of this inscription.

80 Etymologically "he who holds the beginning, the first (place)". See Henning 1953, p. 135 ff.

81 Both IPa and IMP come from **pāti-nāma(n-)*, see Back 1978, p. 249: "Eher liegt im Pal eine (...) Verschreibung von *š* statt *t* vor."

82 For the etymon of this word, see Skjærvø 1983c, p. 58.

83 For its etymon, see Gignoux 1972a, p. 61 (fn. 91), who compares this word with OP **pati-θai̯ka-*.

84 *Corrig.* Gignoux 1972a, p. 62, †⟨ptyrzmy⟩, for ŠKZ 3. About ⟨ptydymn⟩, see Henning 1958, p. 62 (fn. 3); Back 1978, p. 292 and fn. 160; and Huyse 1999,

⟨[p](t)yrzmn⟩[85] *paderazmān* "battle" NPi 12 b2,06; ⟨ptykws⟩ *pādgōs* "region" NPi 33 f14,03 (MPa ⟨p'dgws⟩); ⟨ptykwspn⟩ *pādgōsbān* "governor of the district" ŠKZ 3; ⟨rbysyp⟩ **rabēsēf* "prefect"[86] ŠKZ 11; ⟨rzpn⟩ *razbān* "protector of the vineyard" Nisā 148/2, 149/2, 1651/3, 1874/11 (cf. MMP ⟨rz⟩ *raz* "vineyard"); ⟨s'rr⟩ *sār(d)ār* "leader" ŠKZ 11, 27 (MPa ⟨s'rd'r⟩); ⟨sps⟩[87] *(i)spās* "service" NPi 43 g16,07 (MPa ⟨'sp's, 'sp:s, sp's⟩ *aspās/ispās*); ⟨spsyrdr⟩ *safsērdār* "who holds the sword" ŠKZ 27 (cf. MPa ⟨sfsyr⟩ *safsēr* "sword"); ⟨s'ntwr⟩ *sānatōr* "senator" ŠKZ 11; ⟨špstn, špystn⟩ *šabestān* "eunuch" DE 1,3, ŠKZ 28, 29 (cf. IMP ⟨š'pstn⟩); ⟨tgmdr⟩ *tagmadār* "head of the detachment"[88] Nisā N. 280a/4,5; ⟨twsk, twsyk⟩ *tusīg* (*/tuhīg*?) "empty" Nisā N. 441/1, Nisā 1609/3, 1693/3 (MPa ⟨twsyg⟩); ⟨wr'z⟩ *warāz* (PN) NPi 6 a7,06, 14 c5,02 (cf. IPa ⟨wr'zpty⟩ "chief of the boars", ZMP ⟨wl'c⟩ *warāz* "boar"); ⟨whykr⟩[89] *wehgār* "benefactor" NPi 35 f12,05 (cf. IMP ⟨whyk'lyhy⟩); ⟨wrty'z⟩ *wardyāz* "loot" ŠKZ 5, 12 (cf. IMP ⟨wlty'c⟩)[90]; ⟨wyš't⟩ *wišād* "opened" NPi 23 d3,05 (MPa ⟨wš'd, wyš''d⟩); ⟨[z]mn⟩ *žamān* "time" NPi 40 g7,04 (MPa ⟨jm'n, jm''n⟩); ⟨zyndnyk⟩ *zēndānīg* "prisoner"[91] ŠKZ 28 (cf. MPa ⟨zynd'n⟩ "prison", MMP ⟨zynd'nyg⟩ "prisoner").

b. Patronymics

The numerous patronymics ending in *-(g)ān* belong to the polysyllables with a long final syllable *natura*. These patronymics do not usually have -y#: ⟨'hwptkn⟩ *axubādgān* "sons of Axubād" DE 1,2; ⟨'ndykn⟩ *andīgān* "sons of Andīg" (family name) ŠKZ 23, 25; ⟨'rtbnwkn⟩[92] *ardabāngān* "sons of

---

Band 1, p. 25-26.

85 *Corrig.* Gignoux 1972a, p. 62, †⟨ptyrzmy⟩, for NPi 12 b2,06. About ⟨[p](t)yrzmn⟩, see Skjærvø 1983c, p. 64.

86 The Greek version provides ΕΠΑΡΧΟΣ (= Lat. *praefectus praetorium*). The form ⟨rbysyp⟩ could be an Aramaean loanword in Inscriptional Parthian, see Huyse 1999, Band 2, p. 85.

87 This form is transliterated by Gignoux 1972a, p. 63, as †⟨spsy⟩ "reconnaissance", but the final -y# is not readable, cf. Humbach and Skjærvø 1980, NPi 43 g16, 07 ⟨sps[y]⟩.

88 The first element is Gr. ΤΑΓΜΑ.

89 Gignoux 1972a, p. 66, transliterates †⟨whygr⟩, which has to be changed to ⟨whykr⟩ (see Skjærvø 1983c, p. 113).

90 It would come from **u̯artai̯-āza-* (Back 1978, p. 271).

91 Gignoux 1972a, p. 68: "(gardien ?) de prison", but see Huyse 1999, Band 2, p. 171.

92 11x ⟨'rtbnwkn⟩, but 7x ⟨'rtbnwkny⟩ (3x ⟨['rtb]nwkny⟩, 3x ⟨'rtbn[w]kny⟩). It needs to be investigated whether the forms ending in ⟨-n⟩ and ⟨-ny⟩ are always

Ardabān" Nisā 48/3, 277/1, *et passim*; ⟨ʾrthštrkn⟩ *ardaxšīrgān* Nisā 277/2, 904/3, 1931/4; ⟨ʾsmkʾn⟩ *asmakān* AW 7; ⟨ʾspwrkn⟩ *aspōrakān* ŠKZ 22; ⟨ʾwrnwkn⟩ **orsīgān*[93] ŠKZ 22; ⟨bʾwkn⟩ *bāwagān* DE 1,7; ⟨bndkn⟩ *bandagān* ŠKZ 28; ⟨brdkn⟩ *barragān* ŠKZ 27; ⟨bryskn⟩ *barēsagān* ŠKZ 24; ⟨byltwšn⟩ *bēldūšān* DE 2,4; ⟨bythškn⟩ *bidaxšgān* ŠKZ 28; ⟨dyzptkn⟩ *dizbed(e)gān/ dēzbed(e)gān* ŠKZ 28; ⟨gwtrzkn⟩ *gōtarzgān* Nisā 100/8, 112/4, 660ᵛ/2, 904/12; ⟨hwrkn⟩ *hōragān* ŠKZ 22; ⟨mrtynkn⟩ *mardēngān* ŠKZ 22; ⟨mtrbwznkn⟩ *mihrbōzangān* ŠKZ 23; ⟨mtrdtkn⟩[94] *mihrdādgān* Nisā 1704/1, DE 2,5; ⟨nʾšptkn⟩ *nāšpādgān* ŠKZ 29; ⟨nryshwkn⟩ *narsehgān* ŠKZ 27; ⟨pʾpkn⟩ *pābagān* ŠKZ 20, 23, 25; ⟨pʾsprdkn⟩ *pāsfalgān* ŠKZ 28; ⟨prdkn⟩ *farragān* ŠKZ 22, 24; ⟨prgwzkn⟩ *pērōzgān* ŠKZ 25; ⟨pryptkn⟩ *friyapādgān* DE 2,6; ⟨sʾsnkn, sʾsnykn⟩ *sāsāngān* ŠKZ 28, 29, NPi 14 c1,02, 36 f8,06; ⟨sylwkn⟩ *sēlūkān* ŠKZ 27; ⟨šhypwhrkn⟩ *šābuhrgān* ŠKZ 25; ⟨šnbytkn⟩ *šambīdgān* ŠKZ 27; ⟨ttrwsn⟩ *tatarōsān* NPi 2 a6,02, 15 c14,03; ⟨twsrgn⟩ *tōsargān* ŠKZ 24; ⟨wrdptykn⟩ **gulbedgān* ŠKZ 28; ⟨wrtrgnptkn⟩ *wahrāmbādgān* DE 2,9; ⟨wyprdkn⟩ *wīfargān* ŠKZ 27; ⟨wysprkn⟩ *wispurgān* ŠKZ 24; ⟨wyznkn⟩ *wēžangān* ŠKZ 23; ⟨ywdmngn⟩ *yōdmanagān* AR 3; ⟨yztptkn⟩ *yazdbādgān* DE 2,8; ⟨zbrkn⟩ *zabrᵉgān* ŠKZ 24.

c. *Oblique plural forms*

Finally, it should be noted that the many oblique plural forms ending in *-ān* (and in a few cases also in *-īn*) never have -y#. I list only a few examples of these forms: ⟨ʾlʾnn, ʾrdʾn⟩ *alānān* "Albanians" ŠKZ 2; ⟨ʾnʾryʾn, ʾnyʾryʾn⟩ *anaryān* "non Iranians" ŠNRb 2, ŠVŠ 5, 11, ŠH 2, ŠKZ 1, 15; ⟨ʾrmnyn⟩ *armenīn* "Armenians" ŠKZ 18, 20, 21, NPi 17 c7,05; ⟨ʾryʾn⟩ *aryān* "Iranians" ŠKZ 1, ANRm 2, ŠH 2, 4, ŠTBq 1, 2, ŠNRb 2, 3, NPi 1 a7,01; ⟨dwšmnyn⟩ *dušmenīn* "enemies" NPi 4 a12,04, 33 f12,03, 38 g15,02 (MPa ⟨dwšmynyn, dwšmnyn⟩); ⟨drykn⟩ *dărīgān* "court's servers" ŠKZ 27 (cf. IMP ⟨dlykʾn⟩); ⟨hsynkn⟩ *hasēnagān* "original, first" ŠKZ 16 (MPa ⟨hsyngʾn⟩); ⟨hwrzmn⟩ *xwarazmān* "Choresmians" NPi 41 g2,05; ⟨nyʾkn⟩ *niyāgān* "ancestors" ŠKZ 16, NPi 22 d3,04, 37 g9,01 (cf. MPa ⟨nyʾg⟩ *niyāg* "ancestor"); ⟨prwmyn⟩ *frōmīn* "Romans, Byzantines" ŠKZ 4, 5, 12, 15; ⟨wyspn⟩ *wispān* "all" NPi 8 b6,02 (MPa ⟨wyspʾn⟩); ⟨rzpnn⟩

---

referred to a plural "the sons of X" or can be used for a singular "the son of X". For a different case *-ø/-y*, see fn.174.

93 Correction made from the form in Inscriptional Middle Persian. See Gignoux 1972a, p. 48, and Huyse 1999, Band 2, p. 125.

94 3x ⟨mtrdtkn⟩ but 7x ⟨mtrdtkny⟩ (Nisā 625A/1, 697/2, 740/1, 1089/2, 1376/1, 1389/3, N.218/2). See fn. 92.

razbānān "protectors of the vineyards" Nisā 636/9, 1089/2; ⟨ztn⟩ *žaʸtān* "olives" Nisā 425 (cf. ZMP ⟨zyt'⟩ *zayt*); etc.

3.2.1.2. Polysyllables with a long final syllable positione

The group of polysyllables with a final long syllable *positione* is somewhat smaller than the previous one. Like the polysyllables with a final long syllable *natura*, they do not accept the -y#:

a. Common nouns

Following common nouns appear: ⟨ʾhwrmzd⟩ *ohrmazd* (PN) NPi 14 c5,02, 6 a7,06 [⟨[ʾhwrm]zd⟩] (MPa ⟨ʾwhrmyzd⟩, cf. IMP ⟨ʾwhlmzdy⟩); *⟨ʾpystpt⟩[95] *abestaft* "rebellious/opressed" NPi 18 c4,06 (MPa ⟨ʾbystft⟩ "put under pressure/ free from harshness"); ⟨ʾrwst⟩ *arwast* "virtue"[96] AR 4; ⟨ʾryʾnhštr⟩ *aryānšahr* "land of the Iranians/Aryans" ŠKZ 1, 3, 16, NPi 5 a14,05, 7 b10,01 and *passim* (MPa ⟨ʾryʾn + šhr⟩); ⟨bthš, bythš⟩ *bidaxš*[97] "viceroy" AR 2, ŠKZ 23, 15, 17, NPi 14 c2,02 (cf. IMP ⟨bthšy⟩); ⟨dpyrwpt⟩ *dibīruft* "head of the scribes [title]"[98] ŠKZ 24; ⟨dstgrb⟩ *$dastg^{i}rb/dastg^{a}rb$*[99] "captivity, captive" ŠKZ 11 (IMP ⟨dstglwby⟩);

---

95 This word and its meaning are uncertain. The transliteration ⟨ʾpystpt⟩ (Gignoux 1972a, p. 46) seems to be wrong. Skjærvø 1983c, p. 73, and Cereti/Terribili 2014, p. 366, transliterate it as ⟨ʾpystpy⟩ (see also Humbach 1978, p. 26, c4). Skjærvø points out that this form may be a misspelt *⟨ʾpystpt/ʾpystpty⟩, stemming from OIr. **upa-stafta-* "oppressed" rather than from **apa-stafta-* "rebellious".

96 Henning 1958, p. 39, pointed out that the etymon of this word is related to OP *aruvasta-* "efficiency, diligence". This word comes from OIr. **ar̥u̯ant-ta-* (cf. Av. *auruuaṇt-* "quick, hero, runner", OInd. *árvan(t)-* "runner"), see Brandenstein/Mayrhofer 1964, p. 106.

97 For its etymon, see Huyse 1999, Band 2, p. 132 f. (with bibliography).

98 The form IPa ŠKZ 24 ⟨dpyrwpt⟩ *dibīruft* (IMP ⟨dpywrpt⟩) should be distinguished from IPa ⟨dpyrpty⟩ *dibīrbed* ŠKZ 28, Nisā 90/7, etc. (IMP ⟨dpyrpt⟩, MPa ⟨dbyrbyd⟩) as the Greek version shows: IPa ⟨dpyrwpt⟩ = Gr. ΔΙΒΙΡΟΥΠΤ, whereas IPa ⟨dpyrpty⟩ = Gr. ΑΡΧΙΓΡΑΜΜΑΤΕΩΣ. MacKenzie 1983, p. 287, considers, though, that Greek ΔΙΒΙΡΟΥΠΤ is just a reflect of a mistake in the Parthian text ⟨dpyrwpt⟩. It does not seem to me likely that the Parthian scribe might have confused such an important title and, evenmore, that the Greek version had followed this mistake. See fn. 149.

99 Huyse 1999, Band 1, p. 37, transcribes *dastgraβ* in Inscriptional Parthian and *dastgraw* in Inscriptional Middle Persian, which would come from OIr. **dasta-grab(a)-* (Back 1978, p. 210). Instead of a full degree, a zero degree is to be preferred *$dastg^{i}rb/dastg^{a}rb$ or *$dastg^{i}rw/dastg^{a}rw$ from

⟨dstkrt⟩[100] *dastgird* "property" ŠKZ 16, 17, 25, 29, 30 (MPa ⟨dstygyrd⟩ *dastegird*); *⟨dwškyrb⟩[101] **duškirb* (?) "ugly" NPi 11 b2,05 (cf. MMP ⟨qyrb⟩ "form, shape"); ⟨hndrz⟩[102] *handarz* "instruction" NPi 10 b8,04 (MPa ⟨ʾndrz⟩); ⟨hzrwpt⟩ *hazāruft*[103] "first minister" ŠKZ 23, 25, NPi 14 c3,02 (IMP ⟨hzʾlwpt⟩); ⟨[hw]nrʾwnt⟩ *hunarāwand* "virtuous" NPi 36 f6,06 (MPa ⟨hwnrʾwnd⟩); ⟨kwšnhštr⟩ *kušānšahr* "the land of the Kušans" ŠKZ 2; ⟨msyšt⟩ *masišt* "greatest, highest" DE 4,5, NPi 5 a6,05, 6 a12,06, 27 e12,03, 28 e4,04, 39 g15,03 (=MPa); ⟨mwdrwrt⟩ **muhrward* "sealed (document)"[104] Nisā 780B/5, 1318/7; ⟨nhwšt⟩ *naxwišt* "first" ŠKZ 3, NPi 26 e12,02, 27 e4,03, 38 g7,02 (MPa ⟨nxwšt⟩); ⟨prškrt⟩ *frašgird* "restoration of the original condition" NPi 40 g6,04 (MPa ⟨fršygyrd⟩); ⟨ptyhštr⟩ *pādixšahr*[105] "contract" ŠKZ 19 (related with MMP ⟨pdyxšr, pdxšr⟩ *padixšar* "honour"?); ⟨ptyshw⟩ *padsax(w)*? "answer" NPi 4 a12,04 [⟨ptysh(w)⟩], 33 f12,03, 34 f7,04, 38 g16,02, 39 g6,03 (MPa ⟨pswx⟩ *passox*); ⟨pwhrypwhr⟩ *puhr*ᵉ*puhr* "grandson" ŠH 4, ŠTBq 3, BM 4, 18; ⟨trkpyšn⟩ **tarkafišn*[106] "surplus" ŠKZ 19 (cf. IMP ⟨tlykpyšyn⟩); ⟨wyndršn⟩ *windārišn* "establishment" ŠKZ 17 (cf. IMP ⟨wndršny⟩); ⟨wymnd⟩ *wimand* "limit, frontier" NPi 10 b7,04 (=MPa).

b. Past participles

The bulk of the past participles usually ending in *-V̆C-t* (or *-V̆C-d*) belong to the group of words that end in a final long syllable *positione*. Since Inscriptional Parthian past participles are mostly Aramaeographic forms (see 1.2), the list of phonographic past participles is somewhat limited: ⟨ʾphršt⟩ **abaxrašt* (?) "neglected" Nisā 447/2, 556/2, 661/2, 676/2, 1409/4, 1411/5; ⟨ʾphšt⟩ *abaxšt*[107] "neglected" Nisā 31/9, 525/7, 649/5, 916/6; ⟨ʾtrwht⟩

OIr. **dasta-gr̥ba-* (cf. Huyse 2003, p. 41 [fn. 51], who considers **dasta-gr̥ba-* the origin of IMP ⟨dstglwby⟩).

100 5x ⟨dstkrt⟩, but 1x ⟨dstkrty⟩ (NPi 3 a14,03).

101 *Sic* Gignoux 1972a, p. 50. Skjærvø 1983b, p. 84; 1983c, p. 62, transcribes ⟨ʾwškʾrk⟩ meaning "openly (?)".

102 Gignoux's 1972a, p. 52, transliteration †⟨hndry⟩ is a mistaken transliteration of ⟨hndrz⟩, see Skjærvø 1983c, p. 61.

103 Henning 1965, p. 81, compares this word with Bact. υαζαροχτο.

104 It could be related to MPa ⟨mwhr⟩ "seal" + ⟨wrt-⟩ "to turn, twist" (?).

105 If one reads *pādixšīr* (Huyse 1999, Band 1, p. 48]), this form corresponds to 3.2.1.1.

106 Back 1978, p. 264, proposed an etymon **tara(h)-kaf-a-šna-*.

107 This word is to be related to MMP ⟨ʾbxšʾy-⟩ "to forgive".

ādurwaxt[108] "kindled by fire" ŠKZ 5, 12 (cf. Sgd. ⟨ʾʾ[t]rwh wγt⟩); ⟨ʾwpdšt⟩[109] *ubdišt*[110] "explained, ordered" ŠH 10, ŠKZ 16, 22 (MPa ⟨ʾbdyšt⟩); ⟨ʾwpst⟩ *ōbast* "fallen (down)" Nisā N. 280a/3 (cf. MMP ⟨ʾwbyst⟩ *ōbest*); ⟨ʾwšyht⟩ **ōšixt* "poured, (over)flowed" Nisā N. 218/7 (cf. MPa ⟨ʾšyxt⟩ *āšixt*); ⟨npwšt⟩ *nibišt*[111] "written" ŠKZ 17 (MPa ⟨nbyšt⟩, cf. IMP ⟨npšty⟩); ⟨n[y]sh[t]⟩ *nisāxt* "prepared, made ready" NPi 31 f2,01 (cf. MPa present stem ⟨nysʾc-, nysʾz:-⟩); ⟨ptšht, ptšhyt⟩ *padšixt* "poured, decanted" Nisā 1188/4, 74/4, 867/1 (cf. IPa ⟨ʾwšyht⟩); ⟨wyhšt⟩ *wihišt* "moved, progressed" NPi 16 c5,04 [⟨whyšt⟩], ŠKZ 4, 9 (cf. MMP present stem ⟨whyz-⟩ *wihēz-*).

3.2.1.3. Polysyllables with a short final syllable

The polysyllables with a final light syllable (short vowel followed by a single consonant) can be classified into the four following groups:

a. With the suffix -ag

The bulk of nouns containing the suffix *-ag* (<**-aka-*) do not have the -y# : ⟨ʾpynyʾpk⟩ *abeniyābag* "not fitting, not suitable" NPi 22 d3,04 (MPa ⟨nyʾbg⟩ "fitting"); ⟨ʾstnbk⟩ *istambag* "tyrannical, oppressive" NPi 20 d13,02 (cf. MMP ⟨ʿstmbg⟩); ⟨ʾwyʾtk⟩ **ōyādag*[112] ŠKZ 11 "the rest, the others"; ⟨[ʾwz]brtk⟩ *uzbardag* "produced, extracted from" Nisā 503/5; ⟨gwnk⟩ *gōnag* "kind, sort, colour" ŠKZ 17, NPi 11 b5,05 (MPa ⟨gwng,

---

108 It has a different origin to IMP ⟨ʾtwrswhty⟩ *ādursuxt* "burnt by fire" and MPa ⟨ʾdwrswg⟩ *ādursōg* "burning fire", which are related to MMP ⟨swc-⟩ *sōz-* "to burn" (ZMP inf. ⟨swhtn'⟩). Szemerényi (*apud* Back 1978, p. 193) corrected IPa ⟨ʾtrwht⟩ by *⟨ʾtrwswht⟩. However, as Huyse 1999, Band 2, p. 56, indicated, there is no reason for this correction. Henning 1948, p. 604-605 (especially in fn. 5) related the Parthian form ⟨ʾtrwht⟩ to the Sogdian expression ⟨ʾʾ[t]rwh wγt⟩ "(...) set on fire". Skjærvø 1976, p. 115 (fn. 14), finally proved that Sgd. ⟨wγt⟩ and IPa ⟨°wht⟩ are connected to the Manichaean Parthian present stem ⟨wxš-⟩ *waxš-* "to be kindled, blaze, to kindle" (the past participle of this verb is not attested in Manichaean Parthian), and he translated Sgd. ⟨ʾ(ʾtr)wh wγt⟩ as "fire was lighted".

109 Gignoux's 1972a, p. 48, †⟨ʾwpdst⟩.

110 It can also be read as *abdišt*. The second element is clearly the zero grade of **dai̯ć-* "to indicate, to instruct", see MacKenzie 1999, p. 79, and Skjærvø 1983c, p. 58, for the interpretation of this preverb.

111 Huyse 1999, Band 1, p. 46, transcribes it as *nibušt*.

112 The word is a *hápax legómenon*. Its meaning is deduced from its Greek equivalent: IPa ⟨ʾwyʾtk⟩ = Gr. ΤΟΥΣ ΛΟΙΠΟΥΣ.

gwnq⟩); ⟨hmk⟩[113] *hamag* "all" Nisā 31/11, 525/8, 649/6, 675/7, 916/7, ŠKZ 2, 3, 5, NPi 36 f12,06, 38 g9,02, 39 g10,03 (MPa ⟨hmg⟩); ⟨hmygwnk⟩ *ham^{e}gōnag* "in the same way" NPi 36 f14,06 (cf. IMP ⟨hmgwnky⟩, MMP ⟨hmgwng⟩); ⟨hsynk⟩ *hasēnag* "original, ancient, primeval" NPi 34 f14,04, 38 g4,02 [⟨hsyn[k]⟩] (MPa ⟨hsyng⟩); ⟨krtk⟩ *kerdag/kardag* "action" Nisā 718/9, 1377 (cf. ZMP ⟨krtk', kltk'⟩); ⟨mrthwmk⟩ *mardōhmag* "men" ŠKZ 15 (MPa pl. ⟨mrdwhmg'n⟩); ⟨k(t)k⟩ *kadag* "house" NPi 6 a12,06 (cf. IPa ⟨ktkhwtwy⟩); ⟨msynk⟩ **masyanag* (?) "bigger (son)" DE 2,7; ⟨nwršt[k]⟩[114] **nōraštag* (?) "new (wine)" Nisā 78/1; ⟨nywng⟩ *nēwānag*[115] "heroic, good, brave" NPi 40 g2,04; ⟨phrk⟩ *pāhrag* "(frontier) guard" NPi 4 a6,04, 9 b12,03 (cf. MMP ⟨p'hrgbyd⟩ *pāhragbed* "master of the watch-post"); ⟨pntnk⟩ *pandānag* "path" Nisā 277/7, 485/7, 1125/7, 1222/6, 1379/7 (cf. MPa ⟨pnd'n⟩ –attested in plural only–); ⟨prwrtk⟩ *frawardag* "letter, epistle" ŠKZ 28, NPi 8 b4,02, 22 d1,04, 23 d1,05 (MPa ⟨frwrdg⟩); ⟨plk⟩ *pillag*[116] "steps, monument" NPi 1 a11,01, 15 c11,03 (MPa ⟨pylg⟩); ⟨ptšhtk⟩ *padšixtag* "poured, decanted" Nisā 1654/3 (cf. IPa ⟨ptšht/ptšhyt⟩); ⟨p(tyrk)⟩ *padīrag* "towards" NPi 15 c9,03 (cf. IMP ⟨pt[y]lky⟩, MMP ⟨pdyrg⟩); ⟨tršpk⟩ **taršpag*[(?)] Nisā 1511/6 and ⟨wytršpk⟩ **witaršpag*[(?)] "vinegar" (?) Nisā 1205/2, N. 218/1; ⟨wgwnk, wygwnk⟩ *wigōnag* "different" Nisā 740/2, 636/4; ⟨znbk⟩ *zambag* "fight, battle" ŠKZ 3, NPi 12 b2,06 (MPa ⟨zmbg⟩).

b. Comparatives/superlatives in -tar/dar, -(is)tar

The comparatives and superlatives in *-tar/dar* and in *-(is)tar* have no -y#: ⟨'sktr⟩ *askādar* "higher, in a higher degree" NPi 35 f12,05, 37 g15,01 (MPa ⟨'sk'dr⟩); ⟨drw[y]štstr⟩ *druwištistar* "very well, totally whole, sane" NPi 35 f14,05 (cf. MPa ⟨drwšt⟩ *druwišt*); ⟨krtknystr⟩ *kardagānistar* "more active (for gods)" NPi 30 e6,06 [⟨hw-krtknystr⟩], 33 f7,03, 35 f6,05 (cf. IPa ⟨krtkny⟩, MPa ⟨kyrdg'n⟩, IMP ⟨krtk'ntly⟩); ⟨ny'pktr⟩ *niyābagdar*

---

113 11x ⟨hmk⟩, but DE 1,1 and 2,11 ⟨hmky⟩.

114 The reference in Gignoux 1972a, p. 59, for Nisā 1151/1 ⟨nwršt[k]⟩ seems unlikely, cf. Diakonoff/Livshits 1976, p. 12, who transliterate *⟨nyršt(n)⟩ (*34 = 1151).

115 If one reads this word as *nēwang*, this form should appear in 3.2.1.2. This word's connection to Manichaean Parthian (and Manichaean Middle Persian) ⟨nyw⟩ *nēw* "good, valiant" was pointed out by Skjærvø 1983c, p. 118.

116 Skjærvø 1983c, p. 20-21: "(…) a loanword in Pa, which has no *l* in inherited words." This word was assumed to come from Middle Indian *pīṭha*, see Henning 1952b, p. 518 (fn. 6).

"more fitting, suitable" NPi 40 g2,04 (cf. MPa ⟨nyʾbg⟩); ⟨prtr⟩[117] *fradar* "prior, better" NPi 5 a6,05, 6 a13,06, 27 e12,03, 33 f7,03, 35 f6,05, 39 g16,03 (MPa ⟨ʾfrdr⟩ *afradar*); ⟨ptyrʾmstr⟩ *padᵉrāmistar* "very happy, peaceful" NPi 33 f2,03, 33 f8,03 (cf. IPa and MPa ⟨rʾm⟩ "happy, peace"); ⟨rʾštstr⟩ *rāštistar* "truer, righter" NPi 30 e4-5,06, 31 f8,01, 33 f6,03 (cf. IPa and MPa ⟨rʾšt⟩ "right"); ⟨twh[m]ykstr⟩ *tōhmīgistar* "of a very good family"[118] NPi 6 a13-14,06 (cf. IMP ⟨twmyktwmy⟩, MPa ⟨twhm⟩ "seed, family"). The only exception (outside Nisā, see fn. 117) is NPi 27 e6,03 ⟨wtr(y)⟩ *wa(t)tar*, see 3.2.2.1a and 4.4.2.2.

c. Compounds with second member -kar *and* -bar

Compounds ending in *-kar* "to make" and *-bar* "to bear" do not have the -y# either : ⟨ʾdywr⟩ *adyāwar* "helper, friend" ŠKZ 30, NPi 16 c2,04 (MPa ⟨ʾdyʾwr⟩); ⟨ʾhmrkr⟩ *āhmārgar* "accountant" NPi 15 c3,03 (IMP ⟨ʾmʾlkly⟩); ⟨dʾtbr⟩ *dādbar* "judge" ŠKZ 24, 29 (MPa ⟨dʾdbr⟩); ⟨gnzbr⟩ DE 1,6, ŠKZ 28 *ganzbar* and ⟨gznbr⟩ Nisā 925/2 *gaznbar* "treasurer" (MPa ⟨gznbr⟩); ⟨h[w]rbr⟩ Nisā 675/6 and ⟨hwrybr⟩ Nisā 649/5 *xurbăr/xwarbăr* "cup bearer" (cf. IPa ⟨hwry⟩); ⟨mdwbr⟩[119] *madᵘbăr* "cupbearer, wine dealer" Nisā 31/8, 48/5 and *passim*; ⟨ptkr⟩ *padkar* "image, statue" SPl A1, ANRm 1, ŠNRb 1, ŠVŠ 4 (MPa ⟨pdkr⟩, cf. IMP ⟨ptkly⟩); ⟨rzkr⟩ *razkar* "vinegrower" Nisā 242/5. *UNCERTAIN*: ⟨ptpr⟩ Nisā 31/5, 51/5 and *passim* and ⟨ptypr⟩ Nisā 133/3 **pādbăr* "stock"[120]; ⟨sygpr⟩[121] **sigbăr* (a type of tax? lit. "(tax) which brings vinegar"?) Nisā 139/2, 149/1.

d. Other nouns with a final short syllable

Following nouns do not accept the -y# either : ⟨ʾtrw⟩ *ādur* "fire" ŠKZ 17, 18, 19, ŠVŠ 2 (MPa ⟨ʾdwr⟩, cf. IMP ⟨ʾtwry⟩; cf. ob.pl. IPa ⟨ʾtrwn⟩); ⟨dyzpt⟩ *dizbed/dēzbed*[122] "lord of the fortress" Nisā 1511/1 (but ⟨dyzpty⟩ ŠKZ 26 and

---

[117] 5x ⟨prtr⟩ (in NPi), but 3x ⟨prtry⟩ (in Nisā 277/6, 658/5, 1379/7). See 4.4.2.2.

[118] Gignoux 1972a, p. 65, restores †⟨[tw]mykstr⟩ "très puissant". The restoration and meaning accepted by Skjærvø 1983c, p. 48, is confirmed by the new block a13 (line 6) published by Cereti/Terribili 2014, p. 362.

[119] 77x ⟨mdwbr⟩ (Nisā *passim*), but 1x ⟨mdwbrʾ⟩ (Nisā 503/6), 2x ⟨mdwbry⟩ (Nisā 792/7, 2081/7) and 7x ⟨mdwbryʾ⟩ (Nisā 49/3, 90/2, 133/7, 867/4, 1318/4, 2042/8, N.240/6). See the Livšic's interpretation of the different endings in fn. 174.

[120] It could have the literal meaning "the things brought under protection".

[121] 2x ⟨sygpr⟩, but 1x ⟨sygpry⟩ (Nisā 1651/4).

[122] The reading *dizbed* can be justified as coming from OIr. **dij(a)-pati-* (cf. OP *didā-*, Modern Persian *diz* and Thracian *–διζα*), but a full grade of the

12x Nisā); ⟨hštrp⟩ *(h)šahr(a)b* "satrap" (ob.pl. ⟨hštrpn⟩) AS 6, DE 4,2, KǰI 2, ŠKZ 26, 27, 28, NPi 15 c2,03; ⟨kysr⟩ *kēsar* "emperor" (IMP ⟨kysly⟩) ŠKZ 3, 4, 9, 11; ⟨y'wr⟩ (normally in ⟨HD-y'wr⟩) *yāwar* "time, occasion" ŠKZ 5, 9, 12, NPi 9 b9,03 [⟨y'[wr]⟩], 19 d9,01 [⟨y'w[r]⟩], 28 e6,04, 29 e5,05 (=MPa).

3.2.2. CLASSIFICATION OF POLYSYLLABLES WITH *-y*

To finish the presentation of the material, there now follows a list of the polysyllabic words with -y#. I have classified the testimonies again according to the weight of the final syllable, i.e., according to the syllable preceding -y#. There are three main groups of words: the polysyllables ending in a light syllable (3.2.2.1), the nouns ending in the abstract suffix ⟨-(y)py⟩ (3.2.2.2), and the polysyllables ending in a long syllable (3.2.2.3).

3.2.2.1. Polysyllables with a light final syllable

The final -y# generally occurs in the polysyllabic nouns ending in a light syllable:

a. Common nouns

Following common nouns have the -y#: ⟨'ksy⟩ *āgas* "apparent, visible"[123] ŠH 9, BM 9 (MPa ⟨'gs⟩); ⟨'pdnky⟩[124] *ab(a)danag* "palace" Nisā 660^{v}/5; ⟨'bdny, 'pdny⟩[125] *ap(pa)dan/ab(a)dan*[126] Nisā 683/6, 764/2,7, 796/1, 904/6, N.240/2 (MPa ⟨'pdn⟩ *appadan*, ⟨'fdn⟩ *afδan*); ⟨'wzbry⟩ *uzbar* "extracted from" Nisā *passim*; ⟨bwmhwty⟩[127] *būmxwad* "the own land"

---

root (from OIr. **daij(a)pati-*) cannot be discarded (cf. Av. *daēza-*, OInd. *dehī́-* and Gr. *τεῖχος*).

123 Gignoux 1972a, p. 45, translates it as "informé", maybe due to a mistaken comparison with ZMP ⟨'k's⟩ and MMP ⟨'g'⟩ *āgā(h)* "aware, knowing". However, the meaning of the passage and its equivalent in Inscriptional Middle Persian, ŠH 10 ⟨pty'k⟩ *paydāg* "visible, obvious", confirm the comparison of IPa ⟨'ksy⟩ with MPa ⟨'gs⟩ *āgas* "visible" (these words might be related to Av. *ā-kā-* "manifestus").

124 1x ⟨'pdnky⟩, but 10x ⟨'pdnk⟩ (Nisā 83/2, 518a/2, 713/2, 1151/2, 1427/3, 1437/2, 1891/8, 1927/2, 1951^{1}/2).

125 Six testimonies definitely have -y#, while only two do not ⟨'pdn⟩ (Nisā 62/6, N.324/2).

126 This word is related to OP **appadan-* (attested the acc.sg. OP *appadānam* only), see Henning 1944, p. 110 (fn. 1), where he also explained the Manichaean Middle Persian word ⟨''ywn⟩ *āywan* "palace". See fn. 187.

127 This word is transliterated by Gignoux 1972a, p. 50, as ⟨bwmhwt[y]⟩. However, the final -y# is clearly visible in the photographic reproduction of Minns 1915,

AW 4;[128] ⟨drwzny⟩[129] *drōžan* "lying, false, liar" NPi 18 c2,06 (MPa ⟨drwjn⟩); ⟨hmky⟩[130] *hamag* "all" DE 1,1, 2,11 (MPa ⟨hmg⟩); ⟨hmyshwny⟩ *ham^{e}saxwan* "agreed, of the same opinion" NPi 16 c1,04 (MPa ⟨sxwn⟩ *saxwan* "word, utterance", cf. IMP ⟨hmshwny⟩); ⟨hnzmny⟩ *hanǰaman* "assembly, congregation" NPi 4 a7,04 (MPa ⟨ʾnjmn⟩ *anǰaman*, cf. MMP ⟨hnzmn⟩); ⟨nybpdny⟩ *nēβap(pa)dan* "good palace" Nisā 660^{r}/4; ⟨prtry⟩[131] *fradar* "first" Nisā 277/6, 658/5, 1379/7; ⟨wtʾwny⟩ *widāwan*[132] "reach of an arrow" ŠH 1, ŠTBq 1, BM 15; ⟨wtr(y)⟩ *wa(t)tar* "worse" NPi 27 e6,03 (cf. IMP ⟨wtly⟩, MPa ⟨wtr⟩, comparative of *wad* (IPa ⟨wty⟩); the -y# is something blurred in the Parthian version, see Figure VIII); ⟨wyšry⟩ *wičir/wičar*[133] "judgement, decision" NPi 29 e12,05

Plate 3: ⟨bwmhwty⟩ (see Fig. VII). Nyberg 1923, p. 302, also transliterated the -y# ⟨bwmhwty⟩ and transcribed the word as *būmxwatāi* "landlord, landowner".

128 It is possible to read ⟨bwmhwty⟩ as *būmxwadāy* "landlord" (see the previous footnote). However, the word for "lord" is written ⟨hwtwy⟩ in Inscriptional Parthian (cf. MPa ⟨xwdʾy⟩).

129 The transliteration ⟨drwzny⟩ provided by Skjærvø 1983b, p. 55; 1983c, p. 95, is preferable to Humbach/Skjærvø's 1980, NPi 26 e10,02 ⟨drwzn[p]y⟩, and Gignoux's 1972a, p. 50, ⟨drwznypy⟩.

130 2x ⟨hmky⟩, but 11x ⟨hmk⟩, see the testimonies in 3.2.1.3.

131 3x ⟨prtry⟩, but in NPi 5x ⟨prtr⟩, see the testimonies in 3.2.1.3b.

132 MacKenzie 1999, p. 78, pointed out that the root IIr. **tau̯-* is not attested with long root grade. He therefore rejected the derivation from **u̯i-tāu̯ana-* suggested by Nyberg (*apud* MacKenzie [*ibid.*]). MacKenzie considered that the etymology proposed by Klíma (*apud* MacKenzie [*ibid.*]) was more feasible: **u̯i-tā-u̯ana-* (cf. OInd. *vitan-* "to draw a bow"). However, the long vowel remains unexplained if one thinks of the root IE **ten-* (cf. Lat. *tendō*). I believe that the etymology of *widāwan* is related to OInd. *vídhyati* "to reach with a projectile/to fix in the distance", with the meaning of "to knock in, to fix": IE **u̯i-d^{h}h$_{1}$-i̯-eti* > OInd. *vídhyati*, IE **u̯i-d^{h}eh$_{1}$-u̯en-* > IPa *widāwan* "the reach done with a projectile".

133 Skjærvø 1983c, p. 104, provided two possible transcriptions of this form, either *wižār* "explanation" = ZMP *wizār,* MPa ⟨wycʾr⟩, or *wižīr* "decision, judgment" = ZMP *wizīr,* MMP ⟨wcr⟩. However, I prefer Durkin-Meisterernst's 2004, p. 358, transcription *wizir*. Korn 2009, p. 203-204, also considers that the vowel of the last syllable was originally short, and that ZMP ⟨wcyl⟩ *wizīr* and Modern Persian *wazīr* (vs. Av. *vīcira-* < **u̯i-či-ra-*) were adjusted to the homophone form ZMP *wizīr* and Modern Persian *guzīr* "remedy" (< **u̯i-čr̥-i̯a-*). For the Parthian transcription with *č*, cf. Korn 2010.

(cf. MMP ⟨wcr⟩); ⟨z'wry⟩ *zāwar* "strength, power" ŠKZ 3, 4, 11 (MPa ⟨z'wr⟩).

b. Compounds with second member ⟨-pty⟩ < *-pati

The compounds with ⟨-pty⟩ < **-pati* have always the -y#: ⟨'hrpty⟩ *ĕhrbed* "teacher-priest" ŠKZ 28 (cf. IMP ⟨'yhrpt⟩)[134]; ⟨'hwrpty⟩ *āxwarrbed* "head groom" ŠKZ 24 (cf. ZMP ⟨'hwl⟩ *āxwarr* "stable"); ⟨'rkpty⟩[135] NPi 7 b5,01 (see IPa ⟨hrkpty⟩ below); ⟨'sppty⟩ *aspbed* "lord of horses" Nisā 525/2, 672/3, 916/3, ŠKZ 25; ⟨'twršpty⟩ **āduršbed* "fire priest" Nisā N. 280b/1; ⟨brypty⟩ *barbed* "lord of the door" ŠKZ 28 (MPa ⟨br⟩ *bar* "door, court", cf. IMP ⟨dlpty⟩); ⟨dpyrpty⟩ *dibīrbed*[136] "chief scribe" ŠKZ 28, Nisā 90/7, 99/5, 2150, 2172/1 (MPa ⟨dbyrbyd⟩, cf. IMP ⟨dpyrpt⟩); ⟨dyhpty⟩ *dehbed* "Landlord" NPi 28 e5,04 (cf. MMP ⟨dyh⟩ "land"); ⟨dyzpty⟩[137] *dizbed/dēzbed* "lord of the fortress" ŠKZ 26, Nisā 183/4, 485/6, 652A/2, 780B/3, 9540/3, 1730/2, 1905/3, 2042/2 (cf. MPa ⟨dyz⟩ "fortress", IMP ⟨dzpty⟩); ⟨grstpty⟩ *grastbed* "chief of the supplies" ŠKZ 24, 28 (IMP ⟨glstpty⟩); ⟨hndrzpty⟩ *(h)andarzbed* "counselor" ŠKZ 27 (MPa ⟨'ndrzbyd⟩, cf. IMP ⟨hndlcpt⟩); ⟨hrkpty⟩ (also ⟨'rkpty⟩) *(h)argbed* "chief of the taxes, duties" NPi 5 a17,05, 9 b10,03, 13 c14,01, 17 c9,05 [⟨(h)rk(p)[ty]⟩], 34 f3,04 (IMP ⟨hlgwpt⟩, cf. MMP ⟨hrg⟩ "tax"); ⟨m'dknpty⟩ *mādagānbed* "title, archivist (?)" ŠKZ 24 (cf. IMP ⟨m'dknpt⟩ *māy(a)gānbed*, Gr. ΜΑΙΓΑΝΠΕΔ); ⟨nhšyrpty⟩ *naxčīrbed* "chief of hunting" ŠKZ 24 (cf. MPa ⟨nxcyr⟩ "quarry, chase", IMP ⟨nhcyrpt⟩); ⟨nywdpty⟩ *niwēdbed*[138] "chief of ceremonies" ŠKZ 22, 24, 26; ⟨prštkpty⟩ *parištagbed* "chief of servants" ŠKZ 27 (cf. MPa ⟨pryšt-⟩ *parišt-* "to worship", MMP ⟨pryst-⟩ "to serve", IMP ⟨plstkpt⟩); ⟨sp'dpty, spdpty⟩ *(i)spādbed* "chief of the army" ŠKZ 24, NPi 14 c10,02 (cf. MPa ⟨'sp'd⟩ *ispād* "army"); ⟨tkrpty⟩ **tagarbed* (?) "cup-bearer" NPi 10 c15,02; ⟨w'šrpty⟩ *wāčārbed* "chief of the market" ŠKZ 28 (IMP ⟨w'c'lpt⟩); ⟨wr'zpty⟩ *warāzbed* "chief of the boars" ŠKZ 29 (cf. IMP ⟨wl'cpt⟩; IPa ⟨wr'z⟩ [PN], ZMP ⟨wl'c⟩ *warāz* "boar"); ⟨zynpty⟩ *zēnbed* "chief of the armour" ŠKZ 24 (cf. MPa ⟨z'yyn, zyn⟩, IMP ⟨zynpt⟩).

---

[134] This word would come from **ai̯θra-pati-*, see Back 1978, p. 197, for a discussion of the Parthian word.

[135] This word does not appear in Gignoux 1972a.

[136] Different to IPa ⟨dpyrwpt⟩ *dibīruft*, see fn. 98.

[137] Totally legible 9x ⟨dyzpty⟩, but 1x ⟨dyzpt⟩ (Nisā 1511/1).

[138] This word comes from OIr. **ni-u̯ai̯d-*, cf. ZMP ⟨nwstn', nwyd-⟩ *niwistan, niwēy-* "to announce, consecrate". See Huyse 1999, Band 2, p. 129 (with bibliography).

3.2.2.2. Nouns ending in the abstract suffix ⟨-(y)py⟩

The next more numerous group in which -y# occurs is constituted by the nouns ending in the abstract suffix ⟨-(y)py⟩ *-īf̆* (MPa ⟨-yft⟩): ⟨ʾdywrpy⟩ *adyāwarīf̆* "help" ŠKZ 29 (MPa ⟨ʾdyʾwryft⟩ *adyāwarīft*); ⟨ʾštpy⟩ *āštīf̆* "peace" NPi 40 g15,04 (cf. MPa ⟨ʾštgr⟩ *āštgar* "peacemaker"); *⟨drwzn[p]y⟩[139] NPi 26 e10,02 and ⟨drwznypy⟩ NPi 2 a7,02 *drōžanīf̆* "falsehood" (cf. MMP ⟨drwznyẖ⟩ *drōzanīh*); ⟨hwtwypy⟩ *xwadāyīf̆/ xwadāwīf̆* "rulership" (and the compound ⟨hštrhwtwypy⟩ "rule, government") ŠKZ 17, 22, 23, 24, NPi 3 a5,03, 5 a7,05, 5 a13,05 [⟨(h)wtwypy⟩], 9 b2,03, 18 c11,06, 23 d13-14,05, 35 f7,05, 36 f7,06 (MPa ⟨xwdʾyft⟩ *xwadāyīft*); ⟨krpkpy⟩ *kirbagīf̆* "good action, goodness" ŠKZ 17, NPi 7 b2,01, 12 b4,06, 24 d9,06 (MPa ⟨qyrbgyft⟩ *kirbagīft*); ⟨prznkpy⟩ *frazānagīf̆* "understanding" NPi 37 g4,01 (MPa ⟨frzʾngyft⟩ *frazānagīft*); ⟨šyrkmkpy⟩ *šīrgāmagīf̆* "friendship" NPi 40 g15,04 (MPa ⟨šyrgʾmgyft⟩ *šīrgāmagīft*); ⟨yʾtsʾrpy⟩[140] *yādsārīf̆* "sorcery" NPi 16 c10,04. *Also in the phonographic complements of the Aramaeographic forms*: ⟨OBDkpy⟩ *bandagīf̆* "servitude, bondage" ŠKZ 2, NPi 13 c1,01, 43 g15,07 (MPa ⟨bndgyft⟩ *bandagīft*); ⟨ΘBpy⟩ *nēwīf̆* "courage" ŠKZ 16, 27, 29 (MPa ⟨nywyft⟩ *nēwīft*).

3.2.2.3. Polysyllables with a long final syllable

Finally, the following words which have a final long syllable *positione* or *natura* do accept the -y#:

a. IPa polysyllables with long final syllable positione[141]

Following nouns have the -y# after a long final syllable *positione*: ⟨ʾyzny⟩ **āyezn* (?) "temple" Nisā 969/2, 1682/2; ⟨mzdzny⟩[142] *mazdēzn* "mazdean" ŠTBq 1, 2; ⟨ptyhty⟩[143] **padext* "escaped" (?) NPi 20 d1,02 (same

---

[139] NPi 26 e10,02 ⟨drwzn[p]y⟩ is transliterated by Gignoux 1972a, p. 50, as ⟨drwznypy⟩. Skjærvø 1983c, p. 95, prefers the reading ⟨drwzny⟩ (see 3.2.2.1 and fn. 129).

[140] The transliteration by Gignoux 1972a, p. 48, as †⟨ʾtsʾrpy⟩ ****adsarīf̆*** "superiority" (< **ati-sāra-*) is no longer accepted, see Skjærvø 1983c, p. 70. IPa ⟨yʾtsʾrpy⟩ (NPi 16 c10,04) < **i̯ātu-sāra-* (cf. IMP ⟨y[ʾ]twkyhy⟩).

[141] The form †⟨ptyrzmy⟩ "bataille" occuring in Gignoux 1972a, p. 62, is a mistaken transliteration. For ŠKZ 3, see the form ⟨(p)tydymn⟩, and for NPi 12 b2,06, see the form ⟨[p](t)yrzmn⟩, both in 3.2.1.1a.

[142] See fn. 79.

[143] About the possible meaning of this obscure form, see Skjærvø 1983c, p. 63-64.

as MMP 〈ʾbdxt〉 *abdaxt* ?); 〈[šʾt]zrdy〉[144] *šādzird* "glad of heart, with a happy heart" NPi 22 d13,04 (MPa 〈šʾdzyrd〉, cf. MPa 〈zyrd〉). Compounds with 〈krty〉 *kird* "done" ŠKZ 4, 16 (MPa 〈qyrd〉): 〈zwdkrty〉 *zōdkird* (masc. PN) NPi 14 c15,02; 〈mtrdtkrty〉 *mihrdādkird* (name of a place?) Nisā 681/4 (but also 3x 〈mtrdtkrt〉 Nisā 485/7, 1609/1, 1693/1); 〈dstkrty〉 *dastkird* "estate, possession" NPi 3 a14,03 (but 5x 〈dstkrt〉 ŠKZ 16, 17, 25, 29, 30).

b. IPa polysyllables with long final syllable natura[145]

The -y# appears after a long final syllable *natura* in the following nouns: 〈krtkny〉 *kerdagān* "action (of cult)" ŠKZ 29, 30 (MPa 〈kyrdgʾn〉); 〈hmkwsy〉 *hamgōs* (?)[146] "together with (the adjacent) region" ŠKZ 5, 6 and *passim*; 〈hštrdry〉 *(h)šahrdār* (MPa 〈šhrdʾ(ʾ)r〉) "governor" ŠKZ 3, NPi 33 f3,03, 34 f7,04, 35 f8,05 (cf. ob.pl. 〈hštrdrn〉 NPi 2 a13,02 [〈(h)štrdr(n)〉], 37 g16,01, 39 g2,03).

3.2.3. Distribution of final –*y* in polysyllabic nouns

This overview allows us to identify the same distribution postulated for the monosyllabic nouns (see 3.1.1).

3.2.3.1. Polysyllables ending in long syllable

Polysyllabic words containing a long final syllable *natura* do not have -y# (3.2.1.1). In these words, the long vowel in the final syllable is indicated through *matres lectionis*, e.g., 〈ʾbdyn〉 *abdēn* (MPa 〈ʾbdyn〉), 〈ʾpʾryk〉 *abārīg* (MPa 〈ʾbʾryg〉), 〈ʾrwʾn〉 *arwān* (MPa 〈ʾrwʾn〉 *arwān* and 〈rwʾn〉 *ruwān*), etc., but must not 〈ʾwstykn〉 *ōstīgān* (MPa 〈ʾwstygʾn〉), 〈ʾwyrn〉 *awērān* (cf. IMP 〈ʾwylʾn, ʾwdylʾn〉), 〈dynr〉 *dēnār* (MPa 〈dynʾr〉).

Polysyllables with a long final syllable *positione* do not take the -y# either, e.g., 〈hndrz〉 *handarz* (MPa 〈ʾndrz〉), 〈msyšt〉 *masišt* (=MPa), 〈nhwšt〉 *naxwišt* (MPa 〈nxwšt〉), 〈prškrt〉 *frašgird* (MPa 〈fršygyrd〉), etc. (see 3.2.1.2). Worth mentioning is IPa ŠKZ 24 〈dpyrwpt〉 *dibīruft*[147] (IMP 〈dpywrpt〉). It needs to be distinguished from IPa 〈dpyrpty〉 *dibīrbed* (IMP 〈dpyrpt〉, MPa 〈dbyrbyd〉), as the Greek version shows:[148] IPa 〈dpyrwpt〉 =

---

144 NPi 22 d13,04. Not attested in Gignoux 1972a.

145 I have not registered the form of Nisā N. 280/2 〈ʾsbʾr[y]〉 *asbār* "horseman", since a final -y# is not readable.

146 See 4.4.1 for a discussion of this form.

147 Cf. IPa 〈hzrwpt〉 *hazāruft* "first minister".

148 Different interpretation in MacKenzie 1982, p. 287.

Gr. ΔΙΒΙΡΟΥΠΤ, whereas IPa ⟨dpyrpty⟩ = Gr. ΑΡΧΙΓΡΑΜΜΑΤΕΩΣ. Huyse 1999, Band 2, p. 140-141, offers a possible explanation for the different evolutions on the basis of the stress: OIr. *dipī́ra-pati- > dibīrbed, whereas OIr. *dipīrá-pati- > *dibīrapt > dibīruft, with syncope of the short post-tonic vowel and assimilation of *a > *u* /_ p.[149]

3.2.3.2. Polysyllables ending in light syllable

Polysyllables with a final syllable with short vowel not followed by two (or more) consonants generally have -y#, e.g.: ⟨ʾksy⟩ *āgas* (MPa ⟨ʾgs⟩), ⟨hnzmny⟩ *hanǰaman* (MPa ⟨ʾnjmn⟩), ⟨zʾwry⟩ *zāwar* (MPa ⟨zʾwr⟩), etc. (see 3.2.2.1). The main group of such words is constituted by compounds with second term in *-bed* (< *°*pati-* "lord"). Whereas compounds with a second element *-bed* in Inscriptional Middle Persian do not usually have the final -y# (Huyse 2003, p. 37-38), they have it in Inscriptional Parthian[150]: ⟨ʾhrpty⟩ *ē̆hrbed* (IMP ⟨ʾyhrpt⟩), ⟨dpyrpty⟩ *dibīrbed* (IMP ⟨dpyrpt⟩), ⟨hndrzpty⟩ *handarzbed* (IMP ⟨hndlcpt⟩), ⟨nhšyrpty⟩ *naxčīrbed* (IMP ⟨nhcyrpt⟩), etc. Although Huyse 2003, p. 37-38 (fn. 38) expounded the presence of -y# in Parthian as "(...) la reproduction historique d'un *-ĭ* ancien dans v.-iran. *-pati-", the presence of -y# is regular according to the established pattern, and does not need to (but can also) be explained as a historical spelling.

3.2.3.3. Exceptions

Although the distribution seems clear, there are three groups of words that seem to be exceptions to the general rule (cf. 3.2.1.3):

a) The numerous nouns ending in the suffix *-ag* (< OIr. **-aka-*): ⟨gwnk⟩ *gōnag* (MPa ⟨gwng⟩), ⟨hsynk⟩ *hasēnag* (MPa ⟨hsyng⟩), ⟨znbk⟩ *zambag* (MPa ⟨zmbg⟩), etc. (see 3.2.1.3a). They almost never have

---

149 Although Huyse did not explain the reason for a different accent, it is possible that **dipī́ra- + páti- > dibīrbed* had the accent on the two members of the compound in order to retain the sense "lord of the writing", whereas **dipīrá-pati- > *dibīrapt > dibīruft*, was understood as a single word (with a single accent) with a non-original meaning "lord". Cf. the different translations in Huyse 1999, Band 2, p. 140: ⟨dpyrpty⟩ "Oberstaatssekretär, Kanzler" and ⟨dpyrwpt⟩ "Geheimsekretär", with reference to MacKenzie 1982, p. 287. See fn. 98.

150 The only exception is Nisā 1511/1 ⟨dyzpt⟩ *dēzbed* "lord of the fortress", but the same word is attested with the expected final -y# thirteen times. Diakonoff/Livshits 1977, p. 61, indicate through a *sic* that the transliteration is ⟨dyzpt⟩ for 642 (= Nisā 1511).

the final -y#, with the exceptions being as follows: Nisā 660v/5 ⟨ʾpdnky⟩ *ab(a)danag* (but 10x ⟨ʾpdnk⟩) and DE 1,1, 2,11 ⟨hmky⟩ *hamag* (but 12x ⟨hmk⟩ (MPa ⟨hmg⟩). On the contrary, they usually have the -y# in Inscriptional Middle Persian (about the particular use of the suffix *-ag* in anthroponyms, which seem not to accept the -y# in order to distinguish masculin from feminin, see Huyse 2003, p. 86.

b) The adjectives in comparative and superlative grade with the suffixes *-tar/-dar* (< **-tara-*) and *-istar* (< **-ist(a)-* + **-tara-*): ⟨ʾsktr⟩ *askādar* (MPa ⟨ʾskʾdr⟩), ⟨ptyrʾmstr⟩ *paderāmistar*, ⟨rʾštstr⟩ *rāštistar*, etc. (see 3.2.1.3b). The only exception is the noun ⟨prtry⟩ *fradar* (cf. MPa ⟨ʾfrdr⟩ *afradar*) < **fratara-* "prior, better" (3x Nisā 277/6, 658/5, 1379/7), which also appears without -y# (NPi 4x ⟨prtr⟩), and the adjective ⟨wtr(y)⟩ *wa(t)tar* (MPa ⟨wtr⟩) < **u̯adtara-* "worse" NPi 27 e6,03 (see 4.4.2.2). On the contrary, they always have -y# in Inscriptional Middle Persian (see Huyse 2003, p. 39).

c) Compounds with a verbal noun as a second term like *°kar* (< **°kara-* "to make") and *°bā̆r* (< **°bā̆ra-* "to bear"), see 3.2.1.3c. The scarcely attested Inscriptional Parthian forms ending in ⟨kr⟩ appear to come from **°kara-*, thus IPa ⟨ʾhmrkr⟩ *āhmārgar* (and IMP ⟨ʾmʾlkly⟩ *āmārgar*) "accountant, reckoner" (cf. ZMP ⟨ʾmʾlgl⟩), IPa ⟨ptkr⟩ *padkar* "image, statue" (MPa ⟨pdkr⟩; cf. IMP ⟨ptkly⟩), ⟨rzkr⟩ *razkar* "vinegrower". Nevertheless, the quantity of the vowel of the compounds ending in *°bā̆r* is far from clear. In Manichaean Parthian, there is *°bar*[151] as well as *°bār*[152], without a clear semantic

---

151 Following compounds with *°bar/°war* appear in Manichaean Parthian: ⟨ʾdyʾwr⟩ *adyāwar* "helper, friend", ⟨bʾrwr⟩ *bārwar* "fruitful", ⟨cšmwr⟩ *čašmwar* "endowed with eyes", ⟨dʾdbr⟩ *dādbar* "judge", ⟨dynʾbr⟩ *dēnābar* "religious, devout", ⟨dynwr⟩ *dēnwar* "religious, devout", ⟨gyʾnbr⟩ *gyānbar* "soul-possesing, living creature", ⟨pdbwswr⟩ *padbōswar* "yearning", ⟨phrbr⟩ *pahr(a)bar* "watchman, guardian", ⟨rwdwr⟩ *rōdwar* "compassionate" (from ⟨rwd⟩ *rōd* "sympathy"), ⟨rzwr⟩ *razwar* "right, judge".

152 Following compounds with *°bār/°wār* appear in Manichaean Parthian: ⟨ʾywʾr⟩ *ēwār* "theft, thieving", ⟨bwrzwʾr, bwrzwʾʾr⟩ *burzwār* "high, height", ⟨dyjwʾr⟩ *dižwār* "harsh, grievous", ⟨hynwʾr⟩ *hēnwār* "flood", ⟨pwnwʾr⟩ *punwār* "food given as alms" (from MPa ⟨pwn⟩ *pun* "service, meritorious act"), ⟨sʾrwʾr⟩ *sārwār* "helmet", ⟨swgbʾr⟩ *sūgbār* "sad, mournful" (from MPa ⟨swg⟩ *sūg* "sorrow, grief"), ⟨šʾhwʾr⟩ *šāhwār* "royal, kingly", ⟨tlwʾr, ṯlwʾr⟩ *talawār* "hall, tabernacle", ⟨tnbʾr, ṯnbʾr, ṯmbʾr⟩ *tambār* "body", ⟨tnwʾr, ṯnwʾr⟩ *tanwār* "body, trunk (of tree)", ⟨wwʾr⟩ *wiwār* "separation", ⟨wyʾwʾr⟩ *wyāwār* "answer, speech" (from the present stem ⟨wyʾwr-⟩ *wyāwar-* "to answer, to say", both in

distribution. Therefore, the quantity of the final vowel can only be established in the words attested also in Manichaean Parthian: ⟨ʾdywr⟩ (MPa ⟨ʾdyʾwr⟩) *adyāwar* "helper, friend", ⟨dʾtbr⟩ (MPa ⟨dʾdbr⟩) *dādbar* "judge", ⟨gnzbr/gznbr⟩ (MPa ⟨gznbr⟩) *ganzbar/gaznbar* "treasurer". The quantity of the vowel remains unclear in all the other forms: ⟨h[w]rbr⟩ and ⟨hwrybr⟩ *xurbā̆r/xwarbā̆r* "cupbearer", ⟨mdwbr⟩ *madubā̆r* "wine dealer", †⟨ptgmbr⟩ *padgāmbā̆r*[?] "messenger" (?).[153] Although these forms do not usually have -y#, we do find it sometimes: ⟨mdwbry⟩ (2x, alongside 77x ⟨mdwbr⟩) and ⟨sygpry⟩ (1x, alongside 2x ⟨sygpr⟩).[154]

I will now seek to provide an explanation for several exceptions to the rule (see 4.4.2.2 for the suffixes *-ag*, *-tar/-dar* and *-istar*, and 4.4.2.3 for the compounds in °*kar* and °*bā̆r*).

3.2.3.4. Explanation of the suffix ⟨-(y)py⟩, ⟨krtkny⟩ *and* ⟨hmkwsy⟩

The abstract nouns with the suffix ⟨-(y)py⟩ (see 3.2.2.2) are apparent exceptions, too. If we keep the traditional reading *-īf* (e.g. Tedesco 1921, p. 199; Henning 1958, p. 96-97; Huyse 2003, p. 85 [fn. 125]; Sims-Williams 2004), from Old Iranian **-i̯a-θu̯a-*[155] (MPa ⟨-ypt, -(y)ft⟩, IMP ⟨-yhy⟩, MMP ⟨-y(y), -y(y)h̲⟩), then we would not expect the presence of -y#.

Therefore, we must examine whether a reading *-if* is also possible.[156] As a matter of fact, the suffix appears mostly as ⟨-py⟩ in Inscriptional Parthian: ⟨ʾdywrpy⟩ *adyāwarī̆f* (MPa ⟨ʾdyʾwryft⟩ *adyāwarīft*), ⟨ʾštpy⟩ *āštī̆f*, ⟨krpkpy⟩ *kirbagī̆f* (MPa ⟨qyrbgyft⟩ *kirbagīft*), ⟨prznkpy⟩ *frazānagī̆f* (MPa ⟨frzʾngyft⟩ *frazānagīft*), ⟨šyrkmkpy⟩ *šīrgāmagī̆f* (MPa ⟨šyrgʾmgyft⟩ *šīrgāmagīft*),

---

Manichaean Parthian and in Manichaean Middle Persian), ⟨xwʾr, hwʾr⟩ *xuwār* "prosperity" (opposite of ⟨dyjwʾr⟩).

153 Gignoux's 1972a, p. 71, reading †⟨ptgmbr⟩ (NPi 41 g5,05) is considered a proper name (read ⟨pgrymbk⟩) by Skjærvø 1983b, p. 117. If the etymon of ⟨ptpr, ptypr⟩ **pādbā̆r* "stock" (lit. "things brought under protection" ?) and ⟨sygpr⟩ **sigbā̆r* (a type of tax ?, lit. "(tax) which brings vinegar" ?) is related to a second element °*bā̆r* (< **°bā̆ra-* "to bear"), we can add these words to this list.

154 Livšic (*apud* Rastorgueva/Molčanova 1981, p. 188) suggested for ⟨mdwbry⟩ a historical genitive singular in *-ē* "of the supplier of wine", different from the nominative singular in *-ø*. See fn. 174.

155 Gauthiot 1916a, p. 74; Henning 1958, p. 97.

156 A reading *-if* < **-θu̯a-* rather than *-īf* < **i̯a-θu̯a-* was assumed by Herzfeld 1935, p. 52 ff., *apud* Sims-Williams 2004, p. 539 (fn. 2).

⟨y'ts'rpy⟩ *yādsārī̆f*. Only three words write the suffix as ⟨-ypy⟩:[157] ⟨drwznypy⟩ *drōžanī̆f*, ⟨hwtwypy⟩ *xwadāyī̆f/xwadāwī̆f* and ⟨hštrhwtwypy⟩ *(h)šahr-xwadāyī̆f/xwadāwī̆f* (MPa ⟨xwd'yft⟩ *xwadāyīft*). In two of these forms, the ⟨-y-⟩ is part of the stem and not of the suffix (*xwadāy-* and *(h)šahrxwadāy-*)[158]. Thus, only the form NPi 2 a7,02 ⟨drwznypy⟩ would justify a reading with long vowel: *-īf*.

If the Parthian suffix is to be read *-if*, it could be derived from **-i-θu̯a-*. Although the Manichaean Parthian forms are generally written with the suffix ⟨-yft, -ypt⟩ (or with two dots indicating the elision of *-y-*),[159] some spellings could also justify a reading with a short vowel in Manichaean Parthian: ⟨dbyrft⟩ *dibīrī̆ft* "scribemanship" (M5815 II Vii7), ⟨hwnsndft̲⟩ *hunsandī̆ft* "contentment" ($_0$M259c+M453c R2), ⟨kyrbgft̲⟩ *kirbagī̆ft* "good action" (M7 I Vi3), ⟨r'štft⟩ *rāštī̆ft* "truth" (M229 Vi13, M285 II Vii22), ⟨š'dft⟩ *šādī̆ft* "happiness" (M315 I R7, M460b Vi5), ⟨wdyftgft⟩ *wideftagī̆ft* "deception" (M267b+M314 Rii23), ⟨wjydgft⟩ *wižīdagī̆ft* "the Elect" (M730 Vi9), ⟨wzrgft⟩ *wuzurgī̆ft* "greatness" (M77 R17, M5263 R5). Thus, the spellings IPa ⟨-py⟩ [⟨-ypy⟩] and MPa ⟨-(y)ft⟩ could be read, respectively, as *-if* and *-ift* (< **-iff* [IPa] < **-iβt* [MPa] < **-ift* [with metathesis[160]]

---

157 The form †⟨'rt'wypy⟩ *ardāwī̆f* (MPa ⟨'rd'wyft⟩ *ardāwīft*) appears in Gignoux 1972a, p. 46, but it seems to be deleted. See Skjærvø 1983c, p. 81: "Pa † *'rt'wpy* Gignoux, Glossaire NPi 26 = 25e?,01 ?".

158 For a reading IPa *xwadāy* and not **xwadāw* (< OIr. **hu̯atāu̯a-*), see 2.1.

159 Instances are numerous in Manichaean Parthian: ⟨'frs'gyft, ''frs'gyft, 'frsg:ft⟩ *āfrasāgīft* "contempt", ⟨'njwgyft, 'njwgf:t⟩ *anjūgīft* "distress", ⟨'z'dyft, ''z'dyft⟩ *āzādīft* "freedom", ⟨'wsnyndyft⟩ *ōsanēndīft* "descent", ⟨bgyft⟩ *bagīft* "gods", ⟨bndgyft⟩ *bandagīft* "servitude", ⟨bwrdyft⟩ *burdīft* "patience", ⟨dbyryft⟩ *dibīrīft* "scribemanship", ⟨dwšmny'dyft, dwšmyny'dyft⟩ *dušmenyādīft* "enmity", ⟨dyjw'ryft, dyjw'r:ft̲⟩ *dižwārīft* "hardship", ⟨hmwdndyft, hmwdyndyft⟩ *hamwadĕ̄ndīft* "belief", ⟨hw'bs'gyft⟩ *huabsāgīft* "docility", ⟨hw'mwjdyft⟩ *huāmuždīft* "compassion", ⟨hwnsndyft⟩ *hunsandīft* "contentment", ⟨kmbyft, qmbyft⟩ *kambīft* "smallness", ⟨kyrbgyft, qyrbgyft⟩ *kirbagīft* "good action", ⟨qyrdg'ryft̲⟩ *kirdāgārīft* "might", ⟨mrdyft⟩ *mardīft* "manliness", ⟨nw'gyft⟩ *niwāgīft* "kindly speech", ⟨nys'gyft⟩ *nisāgīft* "brightness", ⟨pw'gyft, pw''gyft⟩ *pawāgīft* "purity", ⟨r'štyft⟩ *rāštīft* "truth", ⟨sy'wyft⟩ *syāwīft* "blackness", ⟨syzdyft⟩ *sēzdīft* "power", ⟨š'dyft⟩ *šādīft* "happiness", ⟨šrmgyft⟩ *šarmagīft* "shame", ⟨wdyftgyft⟩ *wideftagīft* "deception", ⟨wjydgyft⟩ *wižīdagīft* "the Elect", ⟨wysprxtyft⟩ *wispraxtīft* "having care for all", ⟨wystmbgyft⟩ *wistambagīft* "rebelliousness", ⟨wyšmn'dyft, wšmn'dyft⟩ *wišmenādīft* "joy", ⟨wzrgyft⟩ *wuzurgīft* "greatness", etc.

160 Huyse 2003, p. 85, also considers this metathesis as the most probable

< k*-*iθu̯(a)*-)[161] and would represent the zero grade of the suffix that appears in Middle Persian -*īh* < **ii̯a-θu̯(a)-*.

There are two further exceptions with -y# despite a long vowel in the final syllable. The form ⟨krtkny⟩ (2x) *kerdagān* (MPa ⟨kyrdgʾn⟩) "(ritual) action" may originally be seen as a plural form ("the actions", a new formation from *kerdag* "action" [IPa ⟨krtk⟩] specialized for "the actions [of cult]") or probably as a singular abstract < **kr̥ta-kāna-* or **kr̥ti-kāna-* (Back 1988, p. 45). Its use as a grammatical singular word referring to the "god's cult" is well attested from ancient inscriptions.[162] The presence of the final -y# can be explained as an attempt to distinguish *kerdagān* ⟨krtkny⟩ (grammatically singular "god's cult") from *kerdagān/kardagān* *⟨krtkn⟩ (plural oblique form from ⟨krtk⟩ "action"), but the presence of -y# is not etymologically justified.

For the word ⟨hmkwsy⟩[163] "together with (the adjacent) region", which is well attested in the inscription of Šābuhr I in the Kaʾaba of Zarduxšt, two explanations for its final -y# can be adduced. The word occurs in the construction "proper name (of a city)" + ⟨MHWZA⟩ *šahrestān*[164] + ⟨OM prybr hmkwsy⟩ *ad parbēr hamgōs*[165] (IMP ⟨MN plwʾly KHDE⟩ *az parwār hammis*) where *ad ... hamgōs* (and *az ... hammis*) has the meaning "together with" (cf. Gr. ΣΥΝ). The semantic and phonetic shifts of the root of MPa ⟨ʾgwc⟩ *āgōč*[166] "side, direction", MPa ⟨qws, kws⟩ *kōs* "district, region",

---

explanation for the Manichaean Parthian forms.

161 For the latest description of the evolution of OIr.*-*θu̯-* > IPa -*tf*-, MPa -*δf*- and OIr. *-*θu̯#* > MPa -*ft#*, IPa -*f#*, see Korn 2013, with reference to Sims-Williams 2004.

162 For example, in Inscriptional Middle Persian, KKZ 2 ⟨KBYR kltkʾn (ZY) yzdʾn ʾpzʾdyhy⟩ *was kardagān ī yazdān abzayīh* "much cult of gods was increased", where *abzāyī(h)* is a 3rd singular passive imperfect (see Skjærvø 1997, p. 177-178) and *kardagān* is certainly singular (for a possible interpretation as an oblique singular, see Ferrer-Losilla 2010, p. 90 ff.). More instances of this word in Back 1988.

163 Transcribed as *hamgōs* by Huyse 1999, Band 1, p. 29 ff. It may be related to IPa ⟨ptykws⟩ "region, zone" (see Henning 1933, p. 229, who does not provide an etymon for this word). When dealing with IMP ⟨pʾtkwsn⟩, Back 1978, p. 242, states only that it comes from (plural) OIr. **pǎti-kau̯sānam* (also with reference to Henning 1933, p. 229).

164 Cf. IMP ⟨štrdstn⟩.

165 Huyse's 1999, Band 1, transcription.

166 For the opposition MPa ⟨c⟩, ⟨z:⟩ = *č* (from OIr. **č*) and MPa ⟨j⟩ = *ž* (from OIr. **ǰ* and **ž*), see Korn 2010. It should be noted that after *n*, ⟨j⟩ appears almost

MMP ⟨kwstg⟩ *kustag* "side, direction, district", etc. were studied by Sims-Williams 1979, p. 134-135. If ⟨hmkwsy⟩ of Inscriptional Parthian is related to Sogdian ⟨qwš-⟩ "side (of the body)" (cf. also MPa ⟨frgwš-⟩ *fragōš-* "to put aside") and with Old Indian *kukṣí-* "abdomen, cavity", one may suppose an Old Iranian masculine *i*-stem (Old Iranian) **kuč-si-* > **kuš-si-* > **kus-si-* [through assimilation] > (Proto-Parthian) **kusi-*. The reading of IPa ⟨hmkwsy⟩ would be *hamgus*[167] (< **hama-kučsi-*, with *-s* < **-čs*), and the presence of the final -y# could be explained either as a historical spelling or even, if this stem had already become a thematized stem, as the regular tendency to write -y# in the light stems (see below).

3.3. DISTRIBUTIONAL RULES OF FINAL *-y* IN THE NOMINAL INFLECTION

We may therefore formulate the following distributional rules for the presence or absence of -y# in the nominal inflexion:

a) The -y# is absent in the nouns ending in a final long syllable *natura* or *positione* (3.1, 3.2.1.1 and 3.2.1.2), in the words formed through the suffix *-ag* (3.2.1.3a), in the comparative and superlative forms ending in *-tar/-dar*, *-istar* (3.2.1.3b), and in the compounds with a second verbal element in °*băr* and °*kar* (3.2.1.3c).
b) The -y# appears in the monosyllables (3.1) and polysyllables (3.2.2.1) which end in a final short syllable (with a short vowel not followed by two or more consonants) and in the abstract nouns formed through the suffix ⟨-(y)py⟩ (3.2.2.2).

I cannot offer an adequate explanation for certain exceptions to these rules: ⟨ʾrtbnwkn⟩ (11x, but 7x ⟨ʾrtbnwkny⟩ with "unexpected" -y#), ⟨mtrdtkn⟩ (3x, but 7x ⟨mtrdtkny⟩ with "unexpected" -y#), ⟨ʾpdny⟩ (6x, but 2x ⟨ʾpdn⟩, without expected -y#).[168] Nevertheless, many apparent exceptions can be explained in different ways.

---

consistently (coming from OIr. **č* or **ǰ*). Thus, Korn 2010, p. 420, posits that Parthian *č* and *ž* had a postnasal allophone [ǰ]. For a discussion about the existence of a phoneme *ǰ*, see Durkin-Meisterernst 2014, p. 90 ff.

167 The *scriptio plena* of *u* through ⟨w⟩ appears in some words in Inscriptional Parthian, e.g.: ⟨šhypwhr⟩ *šābuhr* (ŠKZ *passim*, NPi 29 e6,05 [⟨(š)hypwhr⟩]), ⟨swgd⟩ *sugd* (ŠKZ 2), ⟨ʾwrnʾy⟩ *urnā* (ŠKZ 6), ⟨ʾwrhʾy⟩ *urhā* (ŠKZ 9), ⟨pwšt⟩ *pušt* (ŠKZ 17), ⟨°dwhtkyE⟩ °*duxtag* (ŠKZ 20-21), ⟨ʾpwrsʾm⟩ *abursām* (ŠKZ 27), ⟨twsyk⟩ *tuhīg* (Nisā 1609/3,6), etc.

168 See fn. 92.

Many words listed in 3.2.2.3[169] can be explained through "inverse spelling"[170]: ⟨[šʾt]zrdy⟩ *šādzird* (instead of *⟨šʾtzyrd⟩; MPa ⟨šʾdzyrd⟩ and simple ⟨zyrd⟩), ⟨mzdzny⟩ *mazdĕzn* (2x ŠTBq[171], instead of ⟨mzdyzn⟩ [IPa 10x]), ⟨krty⟩ *kird* (in ŠKZ 4 and 16; MPa ⟨qyrd⟩), and some compounds with °⟨krty⟩, like ⟨zwdkrty⟩ *zōdkird* (PN), ⟨mtrdtkrty⟩ *mihrdādkird* (name of a place? 1x Nisā, but also 3x ⟨mtrdtkrt⟩), ⟨dstkrty⟩ *dastkird* "estate, possession" (1x NPi, but 5x ŠKZ ⟨dstkrt⟩). However, inverse spellings across two signs are difficult to justify.

Other exceptions can be explained as "historical spellings"[172]: ⟨ʾyzny⟩ **āyezn* (maybe from OIr. **ā-i̯asni̯a-*), ⟨hštrdry⟩ *(h)šahrdār* (from OIr. **xšaθra-dār(a)i̯a-*).

Thus, only few true exceptions remain: ⟨ʾtrw⟩ *ādur* "fire" (MPa ⟨ʾdwr⟩; see 4.2), ⟨np⟩ *năβ* "family" (MPa ⟨nʾf⟩ *nāf*; see 4.2), ⟨hštrp⟩ *(h)šahr(a)b* "satrap" (pl. ⟨hštrpn⟩; see fn. 188), ⟨kysr⟩ *kēsar* "emperor" (IMP ⟨kysly⟩), ⟨yʾwr⟩ *yāwar* "time, occasion" (=MPa; see 4.4.2.3).[173] The word ⟨kysr⟩ can be excluded from the list, since it is a loanword and, accordingly, it was probably not subject to the rules of Parthian orthography.

---

169 I do not know how to interpret the obscure form of NPi 20 d1,02 ⟨ptyhty⟩ **padext*. See Skjærvø 1983c, p. 63-64.

170 Cf. Huyse 2003, p. 38 (fn. 38).

171 Gignoux 1972a, p. 59, provides the transcription ⟨mzdzny⟩, but ⟨mzdyzn⟩ appears in Back 1978, p. 372. I did not have access to any photograph of ŠTBq.

172 Cf. Henning 1958, p. 64 f.

173 For ⟨krtkny⟩ *kerdagān* "(ritual) action" and ⟨hmkwsy⟩ **hamgōs*? "together with (the adjacent) region", see 3.2.3.4.

4. HISTORY OF THE PARTHIAN NOMINAL INFLECTION

In the final section of this study, I propose a possible history of the Parthian nominal inflection that might explain the attested distribution of -y# in Inscriptional Parthian.

4.1. THE TWO-CASE NOUN SYSTEM

Like Inscriptional and Manichaean Middle Persian, Psalter and the Pahlavi Translation of the Avesta, Inscriptional Parthian and Manichaean Parthian also had a two-case noun system (Skjærvø 1983b, p. 132 ff.).[174]

The plural had a clear formal and functional distinction between the direct case (e.g., *yazd* "the gods") and the oblique case (e.g., *yazdān* "by/of the gods"), as we can see in the following example taken from Skjærvø (*ibid.*):

> **ŠKZ 17**: ⟨**y'zt** LN MN ZK gwnk dstkrt OBDWnt W pty **y'ztn** pwšt⟩ ***yazd*** [pl. direct case] *amā ač ēd gōnag dastgird karēnd ud pad* ***yazdān*** [pl. oblique case] *pušt* (...) "The gods in this way make us their property, and with the help of the gods ..."

Singular direct and oblique cases were formally identical in most instances, but a formal difference still occurred in some kinship nouns. In Inscriptional Parthian, the oblique singular of *pid* "father"[175] (MPa ⟨pyd⟩) appears, e.g., in the following instance:

> **ŠKZ 16**: ⟨ANw LN W **ABYtr** W ny'kn W hsynkn dst[krt] YHWt TME (...)⟩ *kū amā ud* ***pidar*** *ud niyāgān ud hasēnagān dastgird būd ōd* (...) "Where for us and for (our) father and for (our) ancestors and for (our) forebears a property was, there ...".

---

174 A three-case noun system (Nom.sg. *-ø*, Gen.sg. *-ē* and Prepositional *-ī̆* or *-ay*) was assumed by Livšic for the Parthian documents in Nisā (*apud* Rastorgueva/Molčanova 1981, p. 188, and Durkin-Meisterernst 2014, p. 198). See 3.2.3.3, fn. 154.

175 This form was not taken into account by Skjærvø 1983c, p. 133. NPi 37 g9,01 ⟨ABYtr⟩ appears in a somewhat damaged context: ⟨[.... ME?] ABYtr W [ny']kn (...)⟩, but a singular oblique case is certain, see Skjærvø 1983c, p. 115.

An opposition between the direct and oblique case in Inscriptional Parthian also occurs in the pronouns of the first and second person singular: ⟨ANE⟩ *az* (MPa ⟨ʾz⟩) “I” (direct case, from the nom.sg. IIr.**aȷ́ʰam*) vs. ⟨LY⟩ *man* (MPa ⟨mn⟩) “to me” (oblique case, from the gen.sg. OIr.**mana*) and ⟨ANT⟩ *tū* (MPa ⟨tw, t̠w⟩) “you” (direct case, from the nom.sg. OIr.**tū*) vs. ⟨L(Y)K⟩ *tō* (MPa ⟨tw, t̠w⟩) “to you” (oblique case, from the gen.sg. OIr. **tau̯a*).[176]

As in Inscriptional Middle Persian, the distribution of the -y#, although assumed to come from the Old Iranian genitive *-*ahi̯a*, is no longer functional, but only a spelling convention in which the syntactical context had no relevance for the presence or absence of -y#. The occurrence of -y# suggests a generalization of the ancient ending of the genitive singular, i.e., the case which expresses the agent in the past (ergative) constructions would have been used as the single case for the singular inflexion (also for the agentive constructions), at least for the thematic stems.

4.2. REMAINDERS OF THE OLD NOMINATIVE AND ACCUSATIVE CASES[177]

Although the occurrence of -y# suggests the generalization of the old thematic genitive singular case, both for the direct case (singular and plural) and for the singular oblique case, not all Parthian nouns come from the old thematic genitive, as Cantera 2009 has shown for Middle Persian.

Besides the form ⟨ABYtr⟩ *pidar* in Inscriptional Parthian, which cannot come from gen.sg. OIr. **piθrah* (OP *piça*, Av. **piθrō*), but instead from ac.sg. OIr. **pitaram* (Av. *pitarəm*; see Cantera 2009, p. 25), there are other Inscriptional Parthian nouns that cannot come from the old genitive. I will mention just a few examples here.

On the one hand, the old nominative singular may be the origin of some words.[178] The noun IPa ⟨np⟩ *nab/(naβ)* (if this reading is correct) cannot

---

[176] For the disputable distinction between IPa ⟨ANT⟩ *tū* vs. ⟨L(Y)K⟩ *tō*, see Jügel 2014, p. 130 (fn. 12); Jügel forthc., §3.2.4. Not reported in Durkin-Meisterernst 2014, p. 206-207.

[177] The old vocative could underlie forms like IPa <bg> [note the absence of *-y#*] *bag* < **bága* “(oh) god”, see 3.1.2.

[178] The noun ⟨mzn⟩ *mazān* (if this reading is correct) cannot come from the genitive singular OIr.**maȷ́n̥tah* (> Parthian ***maz(a)d*) nor from the accusative singular OIr. **maȷ́antam* (> Parthian ***mazand*), but maybe from a thematization of the ancient nominative singular OIr. **maȷ́ā* (< **maȷ́ānᵗ* [nom.sg. YAv. *maza*] < IIr. **maȷ́ʰants* [cf. nom.sg. OInd. *mahā́n*]), which would yield Proto-Parthian

come from gen.sg. OIr. *náftah (> Parthian **naft) or from acc.sg. OIr. *napā̆tam (> Parthian **nabād), but only from the ancient nom.sg. OIr. *nápā.[179] A remnant of an ancient nominative singular can be found in the compound IPa ⟨ʾtwršpty⟩ *(*)āduršbed* "fire priest": *ādurš°* < nom.sg. **ātr̥š* (Av. *ātarš*). The Parthian demonstrative *hō* "he, that" (IPa ⟨hw⟩, MPa ⟨hw⟩) comes also from an old nominative singular (OIr. **hau̯*; see OAv. *huuō*, YAv. *hāu*, OP *hauv*, cf. OInd. *a-sáu*).

On the other hand, the ancient accusative singular is also assumed to be the origin of other forms, e.g.: IPa ⟨ʾtrw⟩ *ādur* (MPa ⟨ʾdwr⟩, IPa ⟨ʾtrwht⟩ *ādurwaxt*) cannot come from the gen.sg. IIr. **ātras* (> OIr. **āθrah* > Parthian ***āhr*), but from the acc.sg. OIr. **ātr̥m* (cf. Av. *ātrəm*; see Cantera 2009, p. 22); IPa ⟨ʾrwʾn⟩ *arwān* "soul" (MPa ⟨ʾrwʾn⟩ *arwān*) cannot come from either a gen.sg. OIr. **ru(H)nah* or from a nom.sg. OIr. **r̥u̯(H)ā*, Parthian *arwān* must come from the acc.sg. OIr. **r̥u̯(H)ānam* (cf. Cantera 2009, p. 18).

4.3. THE SPREADING OF THE OLD THEMATIC GENITIVE SINGULAR **-ahi̯a*

Although several athematic nouns have more or less survived in Parthian, some forms seem to suggest that the old athematic genitive ending *-ah* was already substituted by the thematic **-ahi̯a* in (late) Old Iranian. This substitution is still observed in (late) Old Persian.[180] At some stage in the history of the Parthian nominal inflection, as well as in Middle Persian, the genitive ending would have spread to all nouns, regardless of their origin and function.

---

nom.sg. **mazāni* (> Pa *mazān*, possibly also from Proto-Parthian accusative singular **mazānu*, gen.sg. **mazānē*). The form, in any case, is not easy to interpret.

179 Note that the absence of -y# in ⟨np⟩ ensures that this form cannot hark back to a thematized genitive singular OIr. ***nápahi̯a* (cf. IPa ⟨rpy⟩ *rab/raβ* < OIr. gen.sg. **rápahi̯a*; IMP ⟨npy⟩, with -y# indicating the short preceding vowel). The long vowel MPa ⟨nʾf⟩, transcribed by Durkin-Meisterernst 2004, p. 237, as *nāf*, is etimologically unexplained.

180 The ablative (quite limited) is, in fact, the only case attested in the thematic stems alongside the nominative, accusative and genitive, from the inscriptions of Artaxerxes onward (Cantera 2009, p. 26). But, since the Old Persian *corpus* is quite small, it could be due to chance, as Thomas Jügel has suggested to me.

4.3.1. The trace of **-ahi̯a*. Differences among Inscriptional Parthian and Inscriptional Middle Persian

The starting point is thus the same for Parthian and Middle Persian, but the conditions for the presence or absence of the trace of this ending are nonetheless different. There are three main differences between the aforementioned Parthian rule (see 3.3) and the rule established by Huyse 2003, p. 63, for Inscriptional Middle Persian:

1) The distribution -y#/-ø# appears in Inscriptional Parthian precisely in the nominal inflexion, whereas Inscriptional Middle Persian also has this alternation in verbal and (several) adverbial forms.
2) The presence or absence of -y# depends on the "weight" of the final syllable in Inscriptional Parthian (if heavy —*natura* or *positione*— the final -y# does not appear, but if light, it does), whereas this distribution is related to the vocalic quantity of the final syllable in Inscriptional Middle Persian (if it has a short vowel, -y# occurred, but if it has a long one, there is no trace of the -y#).
3) The distribution -y/-ø also applies in Incriptional Parthian monosyllables, whereas it does not in Inscriptional Middle Persian.

4.3.2. The role of the weight of the antepenultima and the stress

Huyse 2003, p. 77, pointed out the connection between the weight of the penultima and the role of the stress in order to justify the loss or preservation of the (Proto-)Middle Persian -y#: if the penultima had a long vowel, then it is tonic, and the final ending disappears in the postonic position (n^{x} $\acute{\bar{V}}$ ø), whereas if the penultima had a short vowel, it is then unstressed and the final syllable remains as -y# ($\acute{n}^{x}$ $\breve{V}$ y). However, this rule was not valid for the monosyllabic nouns, which in Inscriptional Middle Persian have -y#, although the stress —unavoidably— falls onto the preceding syllable. Huyse 2003, p. 79, explained the occurrence of -y# in the monosyllabic nouns as a consequence of a secondary stress on the final syllable. This is one of the weakest points in Huyse's explanation of Middle Persian.

By contrast, Back 1978, p. 32 ff., linked the -y# in Inscriptional Middle Persian to a phenomenon similar to the Sogdian rythmic law, according to which Sogdian differentiates between heavy and light stems. Such a division of the stems, according to the word structure, into light and heavy stems is also valid for Proto-Parthian. However, while in Sogdian a heavy stem has at least one heavy syllable (Sims-Williams 1984, p. 213), in Proto-Parthian a heavy stem ends in a heavy syllable (i.e., the syllable preceding the ending has a long vowel —or diphthong— or a short vowel followed by two or more consonants). The (Proto-)Parthian heavy stems lost their formal oblique case fairly early on, whereas the Proto-Parthian light stems preserve it longer, and there is an orthographical trace of it in the use of -y#. As in Sogdian (Sims-Williams 1984, p. 204), the stress is responsible for the different evolution of the heavy and light stems.

4.4. HEAVY AND LIGHT STEMS IN (PROTO-)PARTHIAN: POLYSYLLABLES

In Sogdian, the stress falls onto the stem if it is heavy, but onto the ending if the stem is light. In Proto-Parthian (as well as in Proto-Middle Persian), however, the penultima had an important role for determining the heavy or light weight of the stem.

On the one hand, the establishment of the intensity stress in Pre-Proto-Parthian[181] depends on the short or long weight of the penultima: if it is a heavy syllable, the stress fell onto it (e.g., nom.sg. **āzā́tah*), whereas if it is a light syllable, the stress fell onto the previous syllable (e.g., nom.sg. **dráu̯janah*).

On the other hand, and as a consequence of this intensity stress, post-tonic short vowels were lightened and even syncopated[182] in Proto-Parthian (e.g., the nominative singular **dráu̯janah* would have yielded PrPa **drōžni*[183]). In some polysyllabic nouns with syncope of the short post-tonic vowel, certain Pre-Proto-Parthian light stems would have become, at least partially, Proto-Parthian heavy forms (e.g., nom.sg. **dráu̯janah* [light] > **drōžni* [heavy], but gen.sg. **drau̯jánahi̯a* [light] > **drōžanē* [light]).

As I will show forthwith, the stress always fell onto the final syllable of the stem (except for the genitive plural) in the heavy stems, whereas in the

---

[181] I have used this term for a reconstructed first phase that could be common to Parthian and Middle Persian. So the term could be synonymous with Proto-Western Middle Iranian. Reconstructed forms may be also Old Iranian forms, but the reason for using the term Pre-Proto-Parthian is to separate them from original forms, especially when they differ, e.g., the thematized form (PrePrPa) **jā́u̯ara-* is athematic in Old Iranian (**jā́u̯ar-*).

[182] The main conditions under which the syncope can occur in Middle Persian were established by Klingenschmitt 2000, p. 210: a short post-tonic penultima is syncopated when it stands between a non-obstruent and an occlusive consonant, or between two identical occlusive consonants.

[183] The development of nom.sg. (OIr.) **-ah* > (PrPa) **-i* is suggested only by the existence of the nom.sg. ending ⟨-y⟩ *-i* (?) in the Sogdian light stems. Cantera 2009 also assumes this development, albeit not explicitly, for Proto-Middle Persian.

ancient (Pre-Proto-Parthian) light stems the accent was shifted between the direct and oblique cases.

4.4.1. THE POLYSYLLABIC HEAVY STEMS

For the polysyllabic heavy stems, the situation in Pre-Proto-Parthian was as shown below. I take for example the noun OIr. **āzāta-* (Av. *āzāta-*):

	1st: Pre-Proto-Parthian	2nd: Proto-Parthian	3rd: IPa
Nom.sg.	*āzā́tah	*āzā́ti	*āzād* (IPa ⟨ʾzʾt⟩)
Gen.sg.	*āzā́tahi̯a	*āzā́tē	
Nom.pl.	*āzā́tāh	*āzā́ta	
Gen.pl.	*āzātā́nā̆m	*āzātā́na/-ā́nu	*āzādān* (IPa ⟨ʾzʾtn⟩)

Already in Pre-Proto-Parthian, the stress fell onto the last syllable of the stem both for the direct case (singular and plural) and the oblique singular. This intensity stress caused the weakening of the last syllable of the word, giving **-´-ah* > **-i*, **-´-ahi̯a* > **-ē*, etc. In due course, the last syllable of the word was lost from Proto-Parthian to Parthian due to its post-tonic position. As a consequence of this process, the direct case (singular and plural) and the oblique singular were no longer formally distinguishable. As Cantera 2009 pointed out for Middle Persian, the accusative singular also underwent this process of syncretism: acc.sg. (PrePrPa) **āzā́tam* > (PrPa) **āzā́tu* > (Pa) *āzād.*

4.4.2. THE POLYSYLLABIC LIGHT STEMS

The evolution of the forms in the polysyllabic light stems is quite different. Let us take as a first example the word PrePrPa **jā́u̯ara-*:[184]

	1st: PrePrPa	2nd: PrPa	3rd: IPa
Nom.sg.	*jā́u̯arah	*zā́u̯ri	**zār* (but *zāwar*)
Gen.sg.	*jāu̯árahi̯a	*zā́u̯arē (1st scenario) *zāu̯arḗ (2nd scenario) [*zāu̯árē (3rd scenario)]	*zāwar* (IPa ⟨zʾwry⟩)
Nom.pl.	*jā́u̯arāh	*zā́u̯ra	**zār* (but *zāwar*)
Gen.pl.	*jāu̯arā́nā̆m	*zāu̯arā́na/-ā́nu	*zāwarān* (MPa ⟨zʾwrʾn⟩)

The syncopation of the short vowel in a post-tonic syllable took place only in the direct case from Pre-Proto-Parthian to Proto-Parthian (singular:

---

184 Thematized of OIr. **jā́u̯ar-*, cf. Av. *zāuuar-*.

[PrePrPa] *jā́u̯arah > [PrPa] *zā́u̯ri; plural: [PrePrPa] *jā́u̯arāh > [PrPa] *zā́u̯ra), but not in the oblique singular, since the stress initially fell onto this vowel ([PrePrPa] *jāu̯árahi̯a).

If the reason for the disappearance of *-ē# in the heavy stems was its post-tonic position, then its preservation must be due to its non-post-tonic position in the light stems. However, according to the rule of the antepenultima, the old (Pre-Proto-Parthian) genitive singular always had the stress on the final syllable of the stem (regardless of whether the stem was heavy or light). The problem we face then is how to explain the preservation of the ending in the light stems. At least two different explanations are possible, although one is more likely than the other one:[185]

- *1st explanation*: The genitive singular (PrePrPa) *jāu̯árahi̯a became (PrPa) *zā́u̯arē, either because the law of stress of the antepenultima again prevailed after the evolution of Pre-Proto-Parthian *-ahi̯a to Proto-Parthian *-ē, or as a result of an analogical process through the influence of the singular nominative and accusative having the stress on the root (*zā́u̯ri, *zā́u̯ru). Thus, the final ending could have been preserved in the genitive because it was not immediately preceded by a tonic syllable.
- *2nd explanation*: It is also possible that a Proto-Parthian rhythmic law, similar to the Sogdian rhythmic law, operated in the second phase. According to this law, the heavy stems took the stress on the final syllable of their stems, while the light stems took the stress on the

[185] In Cantera's opinion, a third scenario could be the right one. My assumption of a tonic oblique ending in the Proto-Parthian light stems is based on a comparison with Sogdian, and could be related, as Th. Jügel has suggested to me, to the preservation of some inflectional cases in Kurdish and Zāzāki. Cantera thinks, however, that the stress could have been the same in Pre-Proto-Parthian and in Proto-Parthian, i.e., oblique singular *zāu̯árē (third scenario), which would imply that the stress had no role in retaining the ancient ending (as final -y#) from Proto-Parthian to Parthian, since in this case, as in the polysyllabic heavy stems, the ending would be post-tonic (*āzā́tē = *zāu̯árē). In his opinion, Parthian may have tended to avoid monomoraic final syllables. When the final syllable (ending in the nominal inflection) was apocopated, this apocope would have occurred only when this process did not yield a monomoraic word ending. Therefore, the light stems would preserve the old (bimoraic) ending, whereas the heavy stems, when the ending disappeared, would have a bimoraic or trimoraic word ending. This explanation is also suitable for the monosyllabic nouns, and this tendency towards avoiding a monomoraic word ending could be the reason for the lengthening of some monosyllabic nouns, which in Korn 2009 seem to be the exception (e.g., MMP ⟨cyyd⟩ vs. IMP ⟨cyty⟩ / IPa ⟨šyty⟩ *čīd* ← *čid* ← **čidē*).

ending. In Parthian, the stress shift does not affect all the forms of the inflexion, but only the oblique singular. This is probably because the syncopation in the nominative and accusative did indeed produce new heavy forms with a heavy penultima (nom.sg. [PrPa] **zā́u̯ri* < [PrePrPa] **jā́u̯arah*, acc.sg. [PrPa] **zā́u̯ru* < [PrePrPa] **jā́u̯aram*, but gen.sg. [PrPa] **zāu̯arḗ* < [PrePrPa] **jāu̯árahi̯a*)[186]. The rule can in fact be formulated as follows: the oblique singular ending became tonic in Proto-Parthian after a final light syllable of the stem, but not after a heavy syllable.

Most of the polysyllabic light stems can be explained in the same way. Thus, IPa ⟨drwzny⟩ *drōžan* comes from the genitive singular (<***drṓzan*^{e} < [PrPa]**drṓzanē*/**drōzanḗ* < [PrePrPa] **drau̯jánahi̯a*), since the nomimative singular (PrePrPa) **dráu̯janah* would have yielded (Parthian) ***drōžn*. IPa ⟨°shwny⟩ *°saxwan* also comes from the genitive singular (< [PrPa] **sáhu̯anē* / **sahu̯anḗ* < [PrePrPa] **sahu̯ánahi̯a*), whereas the nominative singular [PrePrPa] **sáhu̯anah*, through [PrPa] **sáhuni* would have yielded (Parthian) ***saxun*?. Other examples: IPa ⟨hnzmny⟩ *hanǰaman* < gen.sg. (PrePrPa) **hamǰamánahi̯a* (nom.sg. **hamǰámanah* > (PrPa) **hanǰámni* > (Parthian) ***hanǰam*^{n}), IPa ⟨wtʾwny⟩ *widāwan* < gen.sg. (PrePrPa) **u̯idāu̯ánahi̯a* (nom.sg. **u̯idā́u̯anah* > (PrPa) **u̯idā́u̯ni* > (Parthian) ***widān*).

4.4.2.1. The case of ⟨yʾzt⟩ *and* ⟨prtw⟩

This rule on the light stems is valid for the bulk of polysyllabic nouns,[187]

[186] Proto-Parthian direct cases **zā́u̯ri*, **zā́u̯ru* and **zā́u̯ra* would have yielded Parthian ***zār* (cf. *zōr* in Middle Persian [MMP ⟨zwr⟩, ZMP ⟨zwl⟩], which is assumed to come from a thematized singular nominative or accusative [PrePrPa **jā́u̯arah* or **jā́u̯aram*]; see Cantera 2009, p. 22 (fn. 9). It is possible that, in due course, an analogy with the direct cases and with the very numerous heavy stems meant that the stress of the oblique singular moved from the ending to the stem: (PrPa) **zāu̯arḗ* > **zā́u̯ar*^{e} > (Pa) *zāwar*. The presence of -y# in IPa ⟨zʾwry⟩ would then be the only evidence for this stage with a stressed ending.

[187] The form ⟨prtry⟩ *fradar* would also come from the gen.sg. (PrePrPa) **fratárahi̯a* (> (PrPa) **frátarē*/**fratarḗ* > **frátar*^{e}), since the nominative singular (PrePrPa) **frátarah* would develop (PrPa) **frát*^{ə}*ri*/**frátri* > ***frad*^{r}; and similarly IPa ⟨wtr(y)⟩ would hark back to **u̯ádtarē*/*u̯adtarḗ* < **u̯adtárahi̯a*. The occurrence of IPa ⟨prtr⟩ may be due to an analogical process with all the other comparatives in *-tar/-dar* (see 4.4.2.2). Similarly, the word ⟨ʾpdny⟩ *ab(a)dan* [or *apadan*]? (6x, but 1x ⟨ʾpdn⟩, cf. MPa ⟨ʾpdn [historical spelling]?, ʾbdn, ʾfdn⟩)

proving that the ancient genitive singular was most frequently the origin of such nouns. Two exceptions[188] to this rule are the nouns ⟨y'zt⟩ *yazd* (< OIr. **i̯azata-*) and ⟨prtw⟩ *pahr(w)* (< OIr. **parθau̯a-*) which may come from a direct case:[189]

	1st: PrePrPa	2nd: PrPa	3rd: IPa
Nom.sg.	*i̯ázatah	*i̯ázti	*yazd* (IPa ⟨y'zt⟩)
Gen.sg.	*i̯azátahi̯a	*i̯ázatē *or* *i̯azatḗ	**yazad*
Nom.pl.	*i̯ázatāh	*i̯ázta	*yazd* (IPa ⟨y'zt⟩)
Gen.pl.	*i̯azatā́nā̆m	*i̯azatā́na/-ānu	*yaz(a)dān* (IPa ⟨y'ztn⟩)
Nom.sg.	*párθau̯ah	*párθu̯i	*pahr(w)* (IPa ⟨prtw⟩)
Gen.sg.	*parθáu̯ahi̯a	*párθau̯ē *or* *parθau̯ḗ	**pahraw/**pahrō*?
Nom.pl.	*párθau̯āh	*párθu̯a	*pahr(w)* (IPa ⟨prtw⟩)
Gen.pl.	*parθau̯ā́nā̆m	*parθau̯ā́na/-ānu	**pahr(a)wān* (IPa ⟨(p)rt(w')[n]⟩)

The reason for the transliteration *yazd* and *pahr(w)* of the spelling ⟨y'zt⟩

would come from a thematized genitive singular (PrePrPa) **apadánahi̯a* (> **apádanē* / **apadanḗ* > **ápadan*ᵉ): this form would justify the spelling *abadan*, as well as *abdan/afdan*. This word is scarcely attested in Old Iranian: only the accusative singular OP *apadāna(m)* (Brandenstein/Mayrhofer 1964, p. 104), which would yield Parthian **ab(a)dān*. As Henning 1944, p. 110 (fn. 1), pointed out, the root may be OIr. **apadan-*. From this root, an Old Iranian nom.sg. **apadā*, acc.sg. *(*)apadānam*, gen.sg. ***apadans* / ***apadanah* / ***apadnah* would be expected. Thus, the only case with a final short vowel in the stem would be the genitive singular. The thematized genitive would have been constructed from (OIr.) **apádanah*: (PrePrPa) **apadánahi̯a*.

188 Regarding IPa ⟨hštrp⟩ *(h)šahr(a)b* (pl. ⟨hštrpn⟩), it may be read as *(h)šahrb* (pl. *(h)šahrbān*), which would come from a thematized nominative singular (PrePrPa) ***xšáθrapah* (> [PrPa] ***hšáhrbi* > *(h)šahrb*), and not from the old athematic nom.sg. (OIr.) ***xšaθrapā́u̯ā*, which would yield Parthian ***(h)šahr(a)bā*, nor from a thematized gen.sg. (PrePrPa) ***xšaθrápahi̯a* > IPa *⟨hštrpy⟩ **(h)šahrab*. A different explanation for IPa ⟨hštrp⟩ could be a thematization of the ancient athematic gen.sg. (OIr.) ***xšaθrapā́u̯atah* into (PrePrPa) ***xšaθrapā́u̯ahi̯a* > (PrPa) ***xšaθrabā́u̯ē* > ***hšaθrau̯ā́u̯ē* (with assimilation of **b(β)* to **u̯*) > **(h)šahrāb* (with *ā* < **-au̯ā́-*). Is IPa ⟨hštrp⟩ to be read as *(h)šahrāb/(h)šahrāw*? The origin of Middle Persian ⟨šsp⟩ *šasab* also remains unclear to me.

189 Since these words had two syllables before the ending of the oblique cases in Proto-Parthian, I have not classified them as monosyllables.

and ⟨prtw⟩ in Inscriptional Parthian (and not **yazad*, **pahraw*) is the absence of the -y#, whereby these forms must be Proto-Parthian heavy stems. MPa ⟨yzd⟩ can be read *yazd* or *yazad* (the latter in Durkin-Meisterernst 2004, p. 376). However, the only argument for a reading *yazad* (or *yazaδ*) is the existence in Modern Persian of *īzad* (< MP *yazad*, IMP ⟨yzdty⟩); see Klingenschmitt 2000, p. 198, who traces *īzad* back to the gen.sg. (OIr.) **i̯azátahi̯a*. Parthian, by contrast, has preserved a direct case in this instance, as happens sometimes in Middle Persian, the old nom.sg./pl., or even the acc.sg. (**i̯ázatam* > **i̯áztu* > *yazd*). Concerning IPa ⟨prtw⟩, its equivalent in Manichaean Parthian has the suffix *-ag*: ⟨phrwg⟩ *pahrwag or pahrawag* (the latter in Durkin-Meisterernst 2004, p. 376). If we want to keep this reading, it can be derived from PrePrPa **parθau̯-**ák**-*, where the stressed suffix **-ak* avoided that **-au̯a-* > **ō* (about this suffix, see 4.4.2.2).

4.4.2.2. The suffixes -ag *and* -(is)tar

The Proto-Parthian rhythmic law did not apply to the transparent formations in *-ag* and *-(is)tar*. These suffixes were not affected by the syncopation.[190] In a form like IPa ⟨gwnk⟩ *gōnag*, -y# would be expected. Notice that in such an instance, only the genitive singular (PrePrPa) **gau̯nákahi̯a* explains the absence of the syncope (since the nominative singular **gáu̯nakah* and the accusative singular **gáu̯nakam*, both would have yielded Parthian ***gōng*).[191] Nevertheless, the final -y# does not occur in this kind of words (see 3.2.1.3a-b). Two possible explanations may be adduced:

1) These forms are recent formations, i.e., the suffixes were productive after the loss of the oblique singular ending **-ē*. This explanation is suitable for the exclusive Parthian comparative/superlative suffix in *-istar*, which is certainly a recent merging of the Old Iranian superlative suffix **-ista-* with the comparative one **-tara-*, e.g., IPa ⟨rʾštstr⟩ *rāštistar* (< **rāšt-* + *-istar*). Note that the comparative forms in *-istar* never have the -y#, while there are some instances of old comparative forms in **-tara-* which have preserved it: ⟨wtr(y)⟩ *wa(t)tar* (NPi 27 e6,03) and problably ⟨prtry⟩ *fradar* (Nisā 277/6, 658/5, 1379/7).
2) The suffixes *-ag* and *-(is)tar* bear the stress from ancient times, that is, in such forms the law of the antepenultima did not apply, and the

[190] Cf. the Sogdian parallel in Sims-Williams 1984, p. 208.

[191] See Cantera 2009, p. 19.

ending was lost, as in the heavy stems: (PrePrPa) nom.sg. **gau̯nákah* and gen.sg. **gau̯nákahi̯a* > IPa ⟨gwnk⟩ *gōnag*, (PrePrPa) nom.sg. **rāštistárah* and gen.sg. **rāštistárahi̯a* > IPa ⟨r'štstr⟩ *rāštistar*.

4.4.2.3. The compound nouns in °bara- *and* °kara-

The second explanation mentioned above is also valid for the compound nouns ending with a second member from the verbal roots °*bara-* and °*kara-* (see 3.2.1.3c), where the law of stress did not apparently apply. A fixed stress would fall onto the verbal root (see the parallelism in Middle Persian and Vulgar Latin in Huyse 2003, p. 81 ff.), and these words were dealt with as if they were heavy stems. Thus, e.g., (PrePrPa) **dāta-bara-* "legislator":

	1st: PrePrPa	2nd: PrPa	3rd: IPa
Nom.sg.	*dā́ta-bárah	*dāt**bári**	*dādbar* (IPa ⟨d'tbr⟩)
Gen.sg.	*dā́ta-bárahi̯a	*dāt**bárē**	
Nom.pl.	*dā́ta-bárāh	*dāt**bára**	

Inscriptional and Manichaean Parthian ⟨y'wr⟩ *yāwar* could be explained in the same way. This form is assumed to come from a haplology of OIr. **i̯āu̯a-* + *-u̯ara-* (Nyberg 1974, p. 226). Parthian *yāwar* cannot come from the nominative singular (PrePrPa) **i̯ā́u̯arah* (yielding Parthian **yār* [cf. MMP ⟨j'r⟩ *ǰār*][192]). Only the genitive singular (OIr.) **i̯āu̯au̯árahi̯a* through (PrePrPa) **i̯āu̯árahi̯a* (> [PrPa] **i̯ā́u̯arē*/**i̯āu̯arḗ*) can explain Parthian *yāwar*, but there is no trace of -y# in Inscriptional Parthian. The absence of -y# could well be explained by considering a fixed stress on the second member of this compound in Proto-Parthian (nom.sg. **i̯āu̯ári* and gen.sg. **i̯āu̯árē* > IPa ⟨y'wr⟩ *yāwar*).

4.5. HEAVY AND LIGHT STEMS IN (PROTO-)PARTHIAN: MONOSYLLABLES

The monosyllabic nouns had a stress fixed on the root for all paradigms in Pre-Proto-Parthian, with only the oblique plural (old genitive plural) having the stress on its ending. Since all Pre-Proto-Parthian endings were immediately post-tonic in the monosyllabic stems, one would expect all Proto-Parthian monosyllables to have completely lost their endings in Parthian (see the first explanation in 4.4.2). Nevertheless, as the monosyllabic stems have the same distribution as the polysyllabic ones, a

---

192 But they occur in IMP ⟨y'wly⟩ and ZMP ⟨y'wl⟩. Could these forms be read *yāwar*?

common explanation needs to be sought for both. Under these circumstances, only the second explanation of the preservation of -y# in the polysyllabic stems makes sense, i.e., a light syllable was followed by an accent shift to the ending (see the second explanation in 4.4.2).

4.5.1. THE MONOSYLLABIC HEAVY STEMS

The monosyllabic heavy stems have a single root syllable containing a long vowel (e.g., IPa ⟨š't⟩ *šād* < OIr. **či̯āta-*), a diphthong (e.g., IPa ⟨wym⟩ *wēm* < OIr. **u̯ai̯ma-*), or a short vowel followed by two or more consonants (e.g., IPa ⟨šyhr⟩ *čihr* < OIr. **čiθra-*); that is, containing a heavy *natura* or *positione* root syllable (see 3.1). The explanation for these forms is the same as for the polysyllabic heavy stems (4.4.1), e.g. IPa *šād* < OIr. **či̯āta-*:

	1st: Pre-Proto-Parthian	2nd: Proto-Parthian	3rd: IPa
Nom.sg.	*či̯ā́tah	*či̯ā́ti	*šād* (IPa ⟨š't⟩)
Gen.sg.	*či̯ā́tahi̯a	*či̯ā́tē	
Nom.pl.	*či̯ā́tāh	*či̯ā́ta	
Gen.pl.	**či̯ātā́nām	**či̯ātā́na/-ā́nu	***šādān*[193]

The loss of the final syllable from Proto-Parthian to Parthian caused the syncretism of the direct cases with the oblique singular, as in the polysyllabic heavy stems.

4.5.2. THE MONOSYLLABIC LIGHT STEMS

The monosyllabic light stems are a very small group of words. Not all the monosyllabic words containing -y# that I have offered in 3.1 are however true light stems. For example, the form ⟨k'ry⟩ *kār* is an old heavy stem where -y# could be a historical spelling, if it comes from OIr. **kāri̯a-* (see 3.1.2). The word IPa ⟨'ry⟩ *ar/er* can also be explained through a historical spelling, probably coming from OIr. **ari̯a-* (cf. IPa pl. ⟨'ry'n⟩ *aryān*).

Thus, the scarce monosyllabic light stems are: ⟨hwry⟩ *xwar/xur* (MMP ⟨xwr⟩ *xur*), ⟨mry⟩ *mar* (MMP ⟨mr⟩), ⟨rpy⟩ *rab/raβ* (MPa ⟨rf, rβ⟩), ⟨šyty⟩ *čid*[194] (cf. IMP ⟨cyt'ky⟩) and ⟨wty⟩ *wad* (MPa ⟨wd⟩). Let us take our paradigm to be the word IPa ⟨rpy⟩ *rab/raβ*, coming from

193 I have not found any examples of the plural of this form either in Inscriptional Parthian or in Manichaean Parthian. It is doubtful whether **či̯ā́tāh* and **či̯ātā́nām* would have ever occurred, as Thomas Jügel has indicated to me.

194 See fn. 60.

(PrePrPa) **rapa-*[195]:

	1st: PrePrPa	*2nd: PrPa-A	3rd: PrPa-B	4th: IPa
Nom. sg.	*rápah	*rabí	*ráb^{i}	*(*)rab* (*⟨rp⟩)
Gen. sg.	*rápahi̯a	*rabḗ	*rabḗ (later *ráb^{ē})	*rab* (⟨rpy⟩)
Nom. pl.	*rápāh	*rabá	*ráb^{a}	*(*)rab* (*⟨rp⟩)
Gen. pl.	*rapā́nā̆m	*rabā́na /-ā́nu	*rabā́n^{u}	**rabān*

The first explanation given in 4.4.2 for the polysyllabic light stems cannot explain the presence of -y# in the monosyllabic light stems. If monosyllabic light stems in Parthian carried the stress in the root (e.g., ***rábi*, ***rábē*), the ending would have been totally lost and, as in the heavy stems, no trace of the final -y# would be expected.

This is why we should seek a further explanation (in 4.4.2) of where exactly the Proto-Parthian rhythmic law applied. As mentioned above, only the oblique singular was a Proto-Parthian light form in the so-called polysyllabic light stems, since the syncopation of the short post-tonic vowel turned most Pre-Proto-Parthian polysyllabic light stems into Proto-Parthian polysyllabic heavy forms. All cases (except for the oblique plural) in the monosyllabic light stems were Proto-Parthian light forms (see Proto-Parthian-A phase above).

According to the Proto-Parthian rhythmic law described in 4.4.2 (second explanation), the stress would have fallen onto the ending in the ancient monosyllabic light stems: (PrPa) ***raβí*, ***rabḗ*, ***rabá* (even acc.sg. ***rabú*). Nevertheless, the fact there is no trace of any case other than the oblique singular (⟨-y⟩) suggests that a further levelling of the stress took place in a moment prior to our extant testimonies (see Proto-Parthian-B phase above).

There are reasons to explain why the stress on the ending of the direct cases (singular and plural) was backtrackted in the Proto-Parthian B monosyllabic light stems:

a) The Proto-Parthian rhythmic law may only have applied to Proto-Parthian endings with a long vowel. That is to say, unlike in Sogdian, where a light stem had the stress on its ending, in Proto-Parthian a light stem would have the stress on its ending only if the ending had a long vowel (gen.sg. *-*ē*, gen.pl. *-*ānu*).
b) The plural oblique case (ancient genitive plural), which had had a stressed ending since ancient times, could have influenced the

[195] It may be a thematized form from OIr. **rapah-*, if this word is to be related to OInd. *rapas-* (Cheung 2007, p. 185).

singular oblique one. Thus, the light stems (both monosyllabic and polysyllabic) would have had a tonic ending on the oblique singular, in contrast with the direct cases, which would have an unstressed ending.

c) It is also possible to infer an analogy of the monosyllabic light stems with the polysyllabic light stems, where the syncopation of the post-tonic short vowel turned the Pre-Proto-Parthian direct cases (ancient light stems) into Proto-Parthian heavy stems.

5. CONCLUSIONS

To sum up, the preservation or loss of Inscriptional Parthian -y# is a direct consequence of the Proto-Parthian stress location, which was governed by the weight of the final syllable of the stem (i.e., according to the syllable preceding the ending). If this syllable was long (*natura* or *positione*), the stress fell onto it, and the post-tonic ending was completely lost: this occurred in the (Proto-)Parthian heavy stems (see 4.4.1 and 4.5.1). Due to this loss, the direct case (singular and plural) and singular oblique case were no longer formally distinguished.

On the other hand, the Pre-Proto-Parthian polysyllabic light stems (see 4.4.2) became a mixed paradigm in Proto-Parthian, due to the weakening and/or syncope of the short post-tonic vowel, whereby a paradigm with an accent-shift emerged in Proto-Parthian:

- the stress fell onto the penultima long syllable in the heavy stems (nominative singular –also possibly accusative singular– and nominative plural, e.g., [PrPa] ***zā́u̯ri*, ***zā́u̯ra* < [PrePrPa] **jā́u̯arah*, **jā́u̯arāh*),
- but on the ending in the old geninitive singular, which still had the same phonological structure as the light stems ([PrPa] ***zāu̯arḗ* < [PrePrPa] **jāu̯árahi̯a*).

The preservation of the final -y# in all polysyllabic Proto-Parthian light stems is the most important (or even the only) evidence of the generalization of the singular oblique case for both the singular and plural direct case.

Maybe due to a secondary backtrack of the stress,[196] the final *-*ē* was also lost in the light stems (because of its post-tonic position), and this is the situation of the nominal inflection from the first Manichaean Parthian texts onward, where the final -y# no longer appears.

There are many similarities between the uses of -y# in Inscriptional Parthian and Inscriptional Middle Persian. In both languages, the connection between the weight of the penultima and the role of the stress must be taken into account. As Huyse 2003, p. 77, stated, Inscriptional Middle Persian preserved the final -y#, since it was not immediately preceded by a tonic

196 I contend there was also a first phase in which the stress fell onto the ending in the old nominative singular and plural of the monosyllabic light stems (see 4.5.2). It was only later on that the backtrack of the stress caused the loss of the ending through a process similar to that which caused the loss of the ancient geninitive singular *-*ē* in the polysyllabic light stems.

syllable (ńˣ V̆ y). However, and to explain Inscriptional Middle Persian monosyllabic nouns, he considered a secondary stress on the ending (Huyse 2003, p. 79). I have postulated a phase in which the stress fell onto the ending in the light stems of Proto-Parthian (parallel to Sogdian light stems), both in monosyllabic and polysyllabic nouns, whose trace would be the preservation of -y#. A later levelling of the stress occurred (ob.sg. **hanǰáman*ᵉ̄) to avoid the accent-shift along one and the same paradigm in the polysyllabic light stems (e.g., rec.sg. **hanǰám*ᵃ*ni*, ob.sg. **hanǰamanḗ*). This levelling eventually led to the loss of the final vowel in the original oblique singular case in the light stems (IPa ⟨hnzmny⟩ *hanǰaman* and MPa ⟨ʾnjmn⟩ *anǰaman*).

Inscriptional Parthian seems to be (graphically at least) much more conservative than Inscriptional Middle Persian concerning the uses of -y#. In both languages, as one would expect, the final -y# does not generally occur in uninflected words (adverbs, conjunctions, prepositions, and particles); however, the Inscriptional Middle Persian adverbs in *-rōn* are usually written ⟨-lwny⟩.[197] Inscriptional Parthian -y# never occurs in the inflected verbal forms (see 1.2), whereas -y# occurs in some phonographic verbal forms in Inscriptional Middle Persian,[198] e.g.: ⟨whycwmy⟩ (NPi 9 B11-12,04), ⟨prmʾywmy⟩ (ŠKZ 24),[199] ⟨plmʾdty⟩ (NPi 43 H7,02), ⟨klyty⟩ (ŠKZ 24). In such forms, IMP -y# has no etymological justification. Moreover, the final -y# in Inscriptional Middle Persian also occurs in infinitives[200], e.g., IMP ⟨bstny⟩ (MNFd 3), ⟨plmʾtny⟩ (NPi 34 F12,05). Since the old ending of the infinitive (PrePrPa) **-tanai̯* would have yielded *-tan/-dan* in both Parthian and Middle Persian, the final -y# is also unexpected. Huyse 2003, p. 88, explains IMP ⟨-tny⟩ assuming that the Old Iranian ending **-tanai̯* was reinterpreted as ***-tanahi̯a*. In addition, the nominal inflection also has two plural (oblique) forms, which are unexpectedly written with -y# in Inscriptional Middle Persian: ⟨mgwny⟩ (KSM 3, KNRb 24, KKZ 2, 5, 7, 10,

---

197 Huyse 2003, p. 71, explains this "anomaly" as follows: "(…) la présence du signe final s'explique sans doute plus facilement si on présume que le composé s'est conformé au simple mp. inscr. *lwny* (pehl. *lwn',* mp. man. *rwn)* /rōn/ 'direction' — le *-y* final, après un nom monosyllabique, étant alors tout à fait justifié".

198 Huyse 2003, p. 89 ff.

199 Huyse 2003, p. 92: "(…) la voyelle de la désinence *-wmy* /-ŏm/ était brève, si bien qu'on peut supposer que, par analogie, les règles d'orthographe pour les noms sont devenues valables pour ces formes verbales aussi."

200 Huyse 2003, p. 88.

11, 14) and ⟨dwšmnwny⟩[201].

As the verbal Inscriptional Middle Persian forms show, it seems that the final -y# was usually used in order to mark a previous short vowel, whereas in Inscriptional Parthian it seems more likely that the use of -y# was almost always related to the word's syllabic structure and its nominal origin.

---

201 In a Middle Persian seal (Gignoux/Gyselen 1982, p. 33).

INDEX OF WORDS

ARAMAIC

AVESTAN (Av.)

BACTRIAN

BALŌČĪ

GREEK (Gr.)

INDO-EUROPEAN (IE)

INDO-IRANIAN (IIr.)

INSCRIPTIONAL MIDDLE PERSIAN (IMP)

INSCRIPTIONAL PARTHIAN (IPa)

KURDISH

LATIN (LAT.)

MANICHAEAN MIDDLE PERSIAN (MMP)

MANICHAEAN PARTHIAN (MPA)

MIDDLE INDIAN

MODERN PERSIAN

OLD INDIC (OIND.)

OLD IRANIAN (OIR.)

OLD PERSIAN (OP)

PRE-PROTO-PARTHIAN (PREPRPA)

FIGURES AND PLATES

Fig. I: IMP ŠKZ 27 ⟨pʾpky⟩ [*Apud* Huyse 1999, Tafel 15].

Fig. II: IMP ŠKZ 26/ 27 ⟨... BREr/ ... pʾpky⟩ [*Apud* Huyse 1999, Tafel 15].

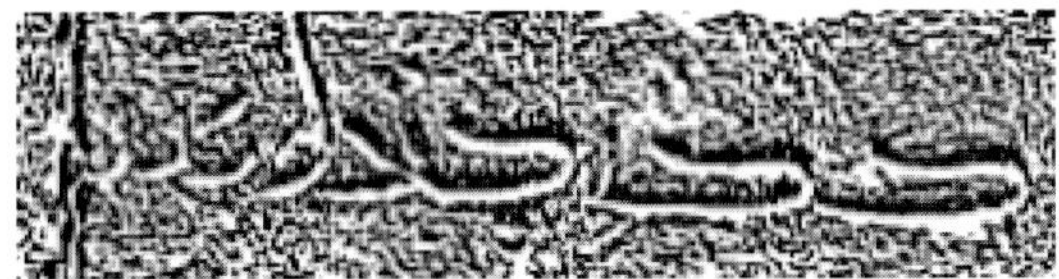

Fig. III: IPa ŠKZ 4 ⟨bybʾlšy⟩ [*Apud* Huyse 1999, Tafel 22].

Fig. IV: IPa ŠKZ 8 ⟨hmkwsy⟩ [*Apud* Huyse 1999, Tafel 22].

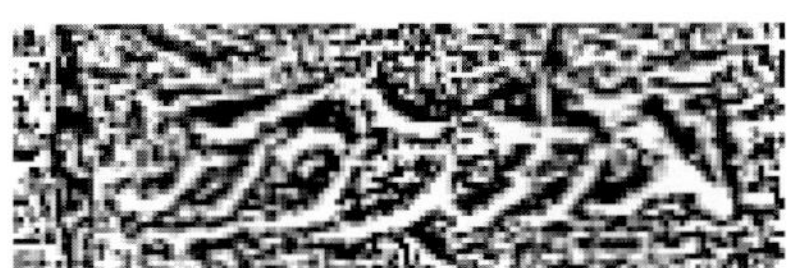

Fig. V: IPa ŠKZ 13 ⟨hmkwsy⟩ [*Apud* Huyse 1999, Tafel 22].

Fig. VI: IPa ŠKZ 24 ⟨mdkdr⟩ [*Apud* Huyse 1999, Tafel 28].

Fig. VII: IPa AW 4 ⟨bwmhwty⟩ [*Apud* Minns 1915, Plate 3].

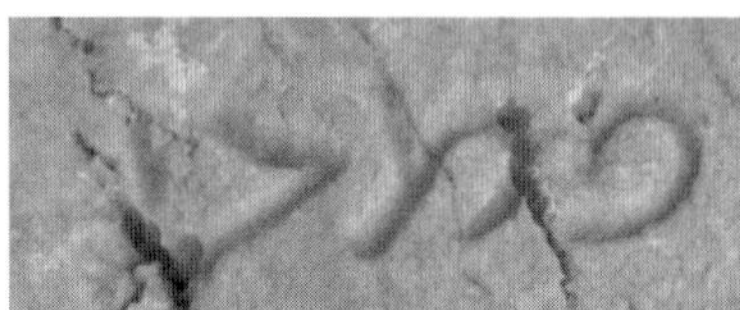

Fig. VIII: IPa NPi 27 e6,03 ⟨wtr(y)⟩ [*Apud* Cereti/Terribili 2014, p. 411, Plate 12]; see block e6 (front cover).

PLATES I-II

Plate I: IPa NPi d11 (Herzfeld's photo) [*Apud* Humbach 1978, Plate 52, fig. 94].

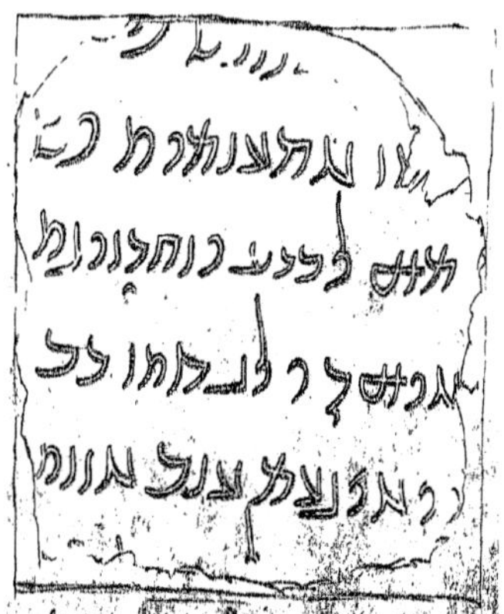

Plate II: IPa NPi d11 (Herzfeld's fac-simile) [*Apud* Humbach 1978, Plate 53.2, fig. 96].

PLATE III

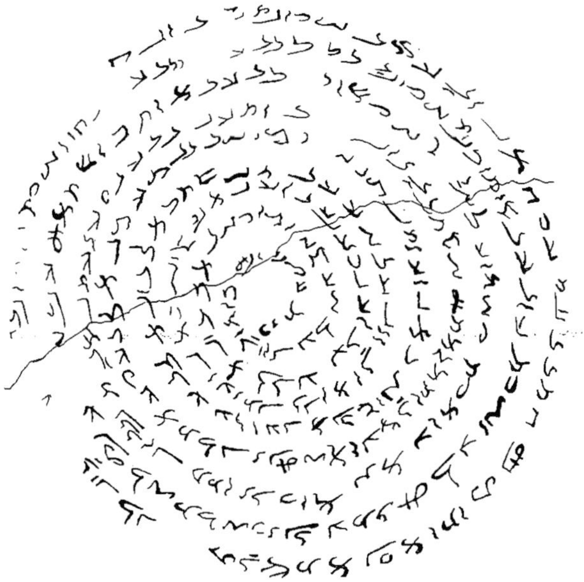

Plate III: Reproduction of the copy of the Hājjīābād Inscription (IPa) in the ceramic bowl of the Babylonian Collection (Yale) [*Apud* Skjærvø 1990: 291].

PLATE IV

Plate IV: Awrōmān parchment [*Apud* Minns 1915, Plate 3].

PLATE V

Plate V: Reproduction of the Kāl-ī-J̌angāl inscription (IPa) [*Apud* Henning 1953, Plate V].

CAHIERS DE STUDIA IRANICA

ISSN 0993 - 8699

Cahier 1 (1982) Ph. GIGNOUX / R. GYSELEN
SCEAUX SASSANIDES DE DIVERSES COLLECTIONS PRIVÉES

Cahier 2 (1984) R. CURIEL / R. GYSELEN
UNE COLLECTION DE MONNAIES DE CUIVRE ARABO-SASSANIDES

Cahier 3 (1985) Jean DE MENASCE
ÉTUDES IRANIENNES

Cahier 4 (1987) Ph. GIGNOUX / R. GYSELEN
BULLES ET SCEAUX SASSANIDES DE DIVERSES COLLECTIONS

Cahier 5 (1986) Ph. GIGNOUX (ed.)
TRANSITION PERIODS IN IRANIAN HISTORY

Cahier 6 (1988) H. DESMET-GREGOIRE / P. FONTAINE
LA RÉGION D'ARAK ET DE HAMADAN : CARTES ET DOCUMENTS ETHNOGRAPHIQUES

Cahier 7 (1989) C.-H. de FOUCHÉCOUR / Ph. GIGNOUX (edd.)
ÉTUDES IRANO-ARYENNES OFFERTES À GILBERT LAZARD

Cahier 8 (1991) Dastur F. M. KOTWAL / J. W. BOYD
A PERSIAN OFFERING. THE YASNA: A ZOROASTRIAN HIGH LITURGY

Cahier 9 (1991) Ph. GIGNOUX
LES QUATRE INSCRIPTIONS DE KIRDĪR. TEXTES ET CONCORDANCES

Cahier 10 (1992) F. M. KOTWAL / P. G. KREYENBROEK
THE HĒRBEDESTĀN AND NĒRANGESTĀN. VOL. I. HĒRBEDESTĀN

Cahier 11 (1992) Ph. GIGNOUX (ed.)
RECURRENT PATTERNS IN IRANIAN RELIGIONS: FROM MAZDAISM TO SUFISM

Cahier 12 (1992) M. SZUPPE
ENTRE TIMOURIDES, UZBEKS ET SAFAVIDES

Cahier 13 (1993) Ph. GIGNOUX / A. TAFAZZOLI
ANTHOLOGIE DE ZĀDSPRAM. Texte traduit et commenté

Cahier 14 (1994) F. de CALLATAŸ
LES TÉTRADRACHMES D'ORODÈS II ET DE PHRAATE IV

[ISBN 2-910640-00-0]

Cahier 15 (1995) J. AUBIN
ÉMIRS MONGOLS ET VIZIRS PERSANS DANS LES REMOUS DE L'ACCULTURATION

[ISBN 2-910640-01-9]

Cahier 16 (1995) F. M. KOTWAL / P. G. KREYENBROEK
THE HĒRBEDESTĀN AND NĒRANGESTĀN. VOL. II. NĒRANGESTĀN

[ISBN 2-910640-02-7]

Cahier 17 (1995) R. GYSELEN
SCEAUX MAGIQUES EN IRAN SASSANIDE

[ISBN 2-910640-03-5]

Cahier 18 (1996) A. S. MELIKIAN-CHIRVANI
LES FRISES DU SHĀH NĀME DANS L'ARCHITECTURE IRANIENNE SOUS LES ILKHĀN

[ISBN 2-910640-04-3]

Cahier 19 (1998) W. FLOOR
THE AFGHAN OCCUPATION OF SAFAVID PERSIA 1721-1729

[ISBN 2-910640-05-1]

Cahier 20 (1998) M. JAAFARI-DEHAGHI
DĀDESTĀN-Ī DĒNĪG. PART I

[ISBN 2-910640-07-8]

Cahier 21 (1999) R. GYSELEN / M. SZUPPE (edd.)
MATÉRIAUX POUR L'HISTOIRE ÉCONOMIQUE DU MONDE IRANIEN

[ISBN 2-910640-06-X]

Cahier 22 (2000) M. PFISTERER
EIN SILBERSCHATZ VOM SCHWARZEN MEER. BEOBACHTUNGEN ZUM GELDUMLAUF IM ACHAIMENIDENREICH

[ISBN 2-910640-08-6]

Cahier 23 (2000) J. AMOUZGAR / A. TAFAZZOLI
LE CINQUIÈME LIVRE DU DĒNKARD

[ISBN 2-910640-09-4]

Cahier 24 (2002) R. GYSELEN
NOUVEAUX MATÉRIAUX POUR LA GÉOGRAPHIE HISTORIQUE DE L'EMPIRE SASSANIDE

[ISBN 2-910640-11-6]

Cahier 25 (2002) Ph. HUYSE (ed.)
IRAN : QUESTIONS ET CONNAISSANCES. VOL. I : LA PÉRIODE ANCIENNE

[ISBN 2-910640-10-8]

Cahier 26 (2002) M. SZUPPE (ed.)
IRAN : QUESTIONS ET CONNAISSANCES. VOL. II : PÉRIODES MÉDIÉVALE ET MODERNE

[ISBN 2-910640-12-4]

Cahier 27 (2002) B. HOURCADE (ed.)
IRAN : QUESTIONS ET CONNAISSANCES. VOL. III : CULTURES ET SOCIÉTÉS CONTEMPORAINES

[ISBN 2-910640-13-2]

Cahier 28 (2002) M. E. SUBTELNY
LE MONDE EST UN JARDIN. ASPECTS DE L'HISTOIRE CULTURELLE DE L'IRAN MÉDIÉVAL

[ISBN 2-910640-14-0]

Cahier 29 (2003) Ph. HUYSE
LE Y FINAL DANS LES INSCRIPTIONS MOYEN-PERSES ET LA 'LOI RYTHMIQUE' PROTO-MOYEN-PERSE
[ISBN 2-910640-15-9]

Cahier 30 (2003) F. M. KOTWAL / P. G. KREYENBROEK
THE HĒRBEDESTĀN AND NĒRANGESTĀN. VOL. III. NĒRANGESTĀN, FRAGARD 2
[ISBN 2-910640-16-7]

Cahier 31 (2005) D. AIGLE
LE FĀRS SOUS LA DOMINATION MONGOLE : POLITIQUE ET FISCALITÉ (XIIIe- XIVe s.)
[ISBN 2-910640-17-5]

Cahier 32 (2005) J. WIESEHÖFER
IRANIENS, GRECS ET ROMAINS
[ISBN 2-910640-18-3]

Cahier 33 (2006) R. GYSELEN (ed.)
CHRÉTIENS EN TERRE D'IRAN : IMPLANTATION ET ACCULTURATION
[ISBN 2-910640-19-1]

Cahier 34 (2007) F. HELLOT-BELLIER
FRANCE - IRAN: QUATRE CENTS ANS DE DIALOGUE
[ISBN 978-2-910640-20-0]

Cahier 35 (2007) É. de la VAISSIÈRE
SAMARCANDE ET SAMARRA : ÉLITES D'ASIE CENTRALE DANS L'EMPIRE ABBASSIDE
[ISBN 978-2-910640-21-7]

Cahier 36 (2008) C. JULLIEN (ed.)
CONTROVERSES DES CHRÉTIENS DANS L'IRAN SASSANIDE
[ISBN 978-2-910640-22-4]

Cahier 37 (2008) M. BERNARDINI
MÉMOIRE ET PROPAGANDE À L'ÉPOQUE TIMOURIDE
[ISBN 978-2-910640-23-1]

Cahier 38 (2008) F. M. KOTWAL / P. G. KREYENBROEK
THE HĒRBEDESTĀN AND NĒRANGESTĀN. VOL. IV. NĒRANGESTĀN, FRAGARD 3
[ISBN 978-2-910640-24-8]

Cahier 39 (2008) É. de la VAISSIÈRE (ed.)
ISLAMISATION DE L'ASIE CENTRALE
[ISBN 978-2-910640-25-5]

Cahier 40 (2009) F. RICHARD / M. SZUPPE (edd.)
ÉCRIT ET CULTURE EN ASIE CENTRALE ET DANS LE MONDE TURCO-IRANIEN, X^e-XIXe SIÈCLES. WRITING AND CULTURE IN CENTRAL ASIA AND THE TURKO-IRANIAN WORLD, 10th-19th CENTURIES
[ISBN 978-2-910640-26-2]

Cahier 41 (2009) V. BERTI
VITA E STUDI DI TIMOTEO I PATRIARCA CRISTIANO DI BAGHDAD
[ISBN 978-2-910640-27-9]

Cahier 42 (2009) Ph. GIGNOUX / C. JULLIEN / Fl. JULLIEN (edd.)
TRÉSORS D'ORIENT. MÉLANGES OFFERTS À RIKA GYSELEN
[ISBN 978-2-910640-28-6]

Cahier 43 (2011) R. GYSELEN / C. JULLIEN (edd.)
« MAÎTRE POUR L'ÉTERNITÉ » FLORILÈGE OFFERT Á PHILIPPE GIGNOUX POUR SON 80e ANNIVERSAIRE
[ISBN 978-2-910640-29-3]

Cahier 44 (2011) C. JULLIEN (ed.)
ITINÉRAIRES MISSIONNAIRES. ÉCHANGES ET IDENTITÉS
[ISBN 978-2-910640-30-9]

Cahier 45 (2011) M. SZUPPE / A. KRASNOWOLSKA / C. V. PEDERSEN (edd.)
MEDIAEVAL AND MODERN IRANIAN STUDIES. PROCEEDINGS OF THE 6th EUROPEAN CONFERENCE OF IRANIAN STUDIES (Vienna, 2007)
[ISBN 978-2-910640-31-6]

Cahier 46 (2011) M. R. JACKSON BONNER
THREE NEGLECTED SOURCES OF SASANIAN HISTORY IN THE REIGN OF KHUSRAW ANUSHIRVAN
[ISBN 978-2-910640-32-3]

Cahier 47 (2011) PH. GIGNOUX
LEXIQUE DES TERMES DE LA PHARMACOPÉE SYRIAQUE
[ISBN 978-2-910640-33-0]

Cahier 48 (2012) A. KRASNOWOLSKA
MYTHES, CROYANCES POPULAIRES ET SYMBOLIQUE ANIMALE DANS LA LITTÉRATURE PERSANE
[ISBN 978-2-910640-34-7]

Cahier 49 (2013) S. AZARNOUCHE
HUSRAW Ī KAWADĀN UD RĒDAG-Ē
« KHOSROW FILS DE KAWĀD ET UN PAGE »
[ISBN 978-2-910640-35-4]

Cahier 50 (2014) P. CALLIERI
ARCHITECTURE ET REPRÉSENTATIONS DANS L'IRAN SASSANIDE
[ISBN 978-2-910640-36-1]

Cahier 51 (2014) A. CANTERA
VERS UNE ÉDITION DE LA LITURGIE LONGUE ZOROASTRIENNE : PENSÉES ET TRAVAUX PRÉLIMINAIRES
[ISBN 978-2-910640-37-8]

Diffusion : PEETERS PRESS, Bondgenotenlaan 153, P.B. 41, B-3000 Leuven.
E-mail : order@peeters-leuven.be